Living the Dream Deferred

LIVING THE DREAM DEFERRED

A Boomer's
Reconnaissance,
Reflection, and
Redemption
On the Road
to Reinvention

R.W. Klarin

Published by Firebird Publishing, Santa Monica, CA 90405
www.firebirdpublishing.com
www.livingthedreamdeferred.com
The author may be contacted directly at rwklarin@yahoo.com

Editorial support: Rick Benzel at Over And Above Creative Group, Los Angeles, CA
Cover design: Jeff Klarin at Bughouse Design, Los Angeles, CA
Interior design: Susan Shankin & Associates
All photographs taken and owned by R.W. Klarin

ISBN: 978-0-9863321-0-4

Printed in United States of America

To the Baby Boomer generation:
May we revive and pursue our youthful ideals of
free expression, community, peace, harmony, adventure,
and love in our elder chapter.

Giving Thanks

Although appearing at the beginning of a book, the note of appreciation is typically written last. And like looking in the rear-view mirror of a car, the objects seem closer or more recent events appear bigger.

So, to avoid that mis-perception, I'll start at the beginning: my mother Belinda Zompa Klarin, who from my earliest days encouraged me to do whatever made me happy. I had a license to explore my interests, which has now become my abiding creed in the post-work chapter. She attended the essay award ceremony in elementary school that marked the beginning of my writing. Along with that guidance, my father Jack Klarin reinforced a contrarian attitude—work hard, but work to live. With that in mind and in pursuit of my innate curiosity, I retired from my career in education at 57—early—so that I could get on with the next chapter, exploring and expressing.

After leaving work and looking for guidance on reinvention, I read many books on the subject. Each had valuable ideas and anecdotes, but it became clear to me that there was no handbook that fit me and my story. I needed to write the book. And writing the book meant I had to work on my skills. That required study and practice and many workshops and conferences in the craft of writing. In that vein, I specifically want to thank Robin Hemley for the inspiration I gained from reading his book on Immersion writing and attending his workshop sessions at Alta, UT.

My close friendships with two other writers, Joe Robinson and Adwin David Brown, provided the guard rails for the treacherous journey of writing the blogs and compiling the book. Joe and Adwin function as a yin/yang for me in writing—craft and form on one hand and authenticity and creativity on the other. Both have been invaluable. Thanks, warrior brothers of the word.

Writing hundreds of pages was in a way the easier part of writing a book. As they say in writing circles, the real writing is in the editing. Congenitally wary of authority figures and a general non-fit at writing conferences, I was determined to find an editor who gets me and what I am writing about. At just the right time, I met Rick Benzel, who provided professional skill and personal empathy to my subject matter. Basically, his support encouraged me to publish the essays in the form you are reading.

Originally just a few personal friends and ultimately thousands of readers of the blog deserve thanks for clicking on and giving their attention to my sometimes confused musings. That kept me going.

Art direction and cover design props go to my brother Jeff Klarin, of *Bughouse*, for reading the hundreds of pages to get the sense of my story and soul. Our conversations around the material honed my own awareness of the message and produced a cover that I totally dig. On the topic of siblings, my sister Karla Klarin, a renowned modern art painter, motivated me to complete this project both through her supportive words and her example as a true *artist*.

I would be remiss to not credit my main teachers on this journey of redemption, expression, and reinvention; Osho (freedom and creativity), the Buddha (mindfulness and impermanence), Baba Muktananda (the infinite nature of the universe), Bob Marley (courage and truth), Werner Erhard (clarity of mind and behavior), and every woman I have loved (heart and feeling).

Finally, much respect goes to Langston Hughes' poem *Living the Dream Deferred.* Although coming out of a different time and culture, his message applies to anyone who gives up on a dream. Surely, we don't want to end up as Lorraine Hansberry depicts in her classic play, *Raisins in the Sun*.

Giving thanks for your time and what is. I hope you enjoy my adventure and get inspired to begin your own. One love!

Introduction

A few years ago I graduated from my career in public high school education and leapt into the unknown, unstructured world called "retirement." I was transitioning from what sociology professor Sara Lawrence Lightfoot calls the second chapter of life—the years after graduating from college and pursuing our careers—and moving into the third chapter. My thirty years as a high school teacher and principal had been fulfilling and rewarding, both financially and professionally. I had what I considered a well-balanced life; Teaching, career development, travel, sports, and a lot of spiritual and personal growth filled my weeks and weekends. But I always yearned for more free time to explore the world and develop new activities and skills.

My retirement came suddenly when I was involuntarily transferred by my employer, the Los Angeles Unified School District. The new position would be a redo of what I had already done. No growth, no learning, and continued frustration with a system that resists original thought and creativity. One of my lasting memories is an incident at a staff development in-service day, when my direct supervisor introduced me by lifting her eyebrows and saying that I was 'innovative.' My frequent creative suggestions for improving our practices were rarely well- received in that culture.

The usual response was the euphemistic, "We'll take that under advisement," or more plainly said, trashed.

I visited a financial counselor who confirmed that I had enough assets to quit working for a living. "You can retire," he told me bluntly. I took a few days off and went to the desert to commune with my deeper self. Somewhere between the long afternoon shadows of the San Jacinto Mountains and the third margarita at Las Casuelas outdoor Mexican restaurant, the answer came clear to me: Yes, it was time to leave the security of work and begin the next phase of my life. At the end of that school year, I turned in my ID card and retired from that role. One of the boldest moves I've ever made.

I had no plan. In the back of my mind I harbored a long nurtured, vague notion that retirement would come naturally, like an extended vacation. I would sleep in late, play tennis, travel, take art classes, go to jazz clubs during the week and stay out till the wee hours . . . just fun, fun, fun. It would be what psychologist Martin Seligman calls experiencing 'pleasurable emotions.'

But living a fulfilling retirement turned out to be a lot tougher than I thought. Retiring is simple to do, but not easy to live. I found myself falling back into long entrenched work habits— I needed to be productive, successful, and in charge. Slowly, I realized a life of indolence and leisure was not enough—and yet I had no idea what my new lifestyle should be. I didn't know how to identify and choose what I wanted to do in my third chapter. I was lost in my own skin, without a road map for translating my newfound freedom into a meaningful life, whatever that could be.

I wallowed in doubt, confusion, and ennui for months. Finally, a close friend noticed my existential angst and said, "Hey, why don't you write a blog? You're not the only one dealing with this."

A light flickered on, illuminating, a path forward. The next day I began posting my new blog, *Living the Dream Deferred*.

I published essays that chronicled my own research, studies, ideas, and experiences on the zigzagging road of my reinvention after retirement for over two years. Like most choices in life, making the commitment to write consistently and share my inner and outer adventures led me to many unexpected places, insights, and growth. Those blogs are the basis of the book you are reading.

In the process of writing, I discovered a totally different terrain than I had expected. If you are anything like me, I think you'll find our Baby Boomer version of retirement is much different than our parent's generation. For most of us, it isn't enough to simply travel, play more golf, get high, and run errands. Many Boomers want more, and making that shift can be tricky. I believe it is all about the dreams—the long-forgotten personal dreams of our youth that we have stored in our subconscious. These dreams don't go away. They have remained submerged waiting for the day when we can resuscitate them. One of the great opportunities of our retirement years is the chance to live out some of those youthful dreams and turn them into reality.

We Boomers are now attaining the age that allows many of us to take the time to hone the clarity of our intentions, and like Carlos Castaneda's Don Juan, shape-shift ourselves. "Someday" has come for our generation, as we move into our senior years. We now have the time to water the long-dormant seeds of creative expression, curiosity, purpose, community, and freedom planted in our youth. Doing so, we nurture ourselves and assume the role of elders who have a valuable legacy to contribute. Forty million Boomers are about to enter—10,000 Boomers turn 65 every day.

In these pieces you'll find an amalgam of reporting, memoir, reflections, and perhaps a smidgeon of self-help. I hope you will find the pieces fit together for you like a mosaic of differ-ent colors that provides a coherent picture of your own conscious reinvention. I do not claim to have answers for everyone, but I do hope to provoke insight and inspire you to find the courage to take your personal journey to creative expression and reinvention.

At the end of each essay, I offer two short exercises—an "inner" and an "outer." I hope these will inspire you to ACT. While I wrote this book because I value writing and reading, I am the first one to tell you that reading about life is not life. Many years ago, in the discipline of general semantics they had a slogan, 'the map is not the territory.' I encourage anyone embarking on the journey to reinvention to take the time to look within yourself and out into your world, not only at default maps (beliefs) or screens. Then go write, paint, or dance—or in some way express the emotions that are bubbling within you. Expression is liberating. Find a medium and dive into the cauldron of creativity.

I invite you join me on this trip of discovery and adventure to an unknown land that lies within and without you. Perhaps your journey will take you across many dark valleys and dry deserts that ultimately lead you up the mountain of life satisfaction. Join me in discovering and listening to the *Muse*. It calls out to brave souls who want to live full-out and leave this life with no regrets.

'He that's not busy being born, is busy dying'
—Bob Dylan

PART 1.
REINVENTION

Chapter 1
Open the Last Door and Wake Up!

*Why do you run around sprinkling holy water? There's
an ocean inside of you and when you're ready, you'll
drink.*   *—Kabir*

The true vocation of man is to find the way to himself.
           —Hermann Hesse

A time of reckoning had arrived, suddenly, banging in my head.

Sixty was a major turning point for me. Inescapable—I was now
one of the older generation. Coming from a generation that
made a cult of youth veneration, this was a tough awakening.
How could I blame the 'old' people? How can I be young when
my body has numerous aches and pain? How do I look for a
soul- mate when my mental pictures are still thirty years old?
How do I find right home when I don't have to commute? In
other words, how do I live my maximum life now that forty
years of adulthood have passed and old dreams are waking up?

Facing this phase of life with honesty, optimism, and joy
presented a different challenge, perhaps more challenging, than
the 'career' phase. The basic needs ruled; making money, build-

ing a professional career, healing neuroses, and buying a home and luxury car—for many marrying and raising a family, and for others traveling the world. And maybe seeking enlightenment. There is more to life than the job or career, but many of us don't know how to begin again. Or as I say, **refire**—as in 'I'm fired up.'

Is my life about playing more tennis and traveling every month? Returning to the old job as a consultant or substitute? Learning to play guitar? Starting a business? Pursuing that long forgotten art? Volunteering for a worthy cause?

Questions such as these vexed me. Shifting into the after-work phase or 3rd Chapter, as one writer calls it, was an opportunity to at last live that long-forgotten dream. Other facets of one's char-acter may have been suppressed by the exigencies and practical aspects of life. Now, there was an opportunity to liberate myself and experience authentic happiness in the final act. Not the 'smiley face' leisure of our parents or grandparents, but the deep satisfaction of completion of inner purpose.

And we continue to be role models for the younger generations who are watching, listening, and learning from us Boomers. We have had an exciting time for the last forty years; let's make the next phase our crowning glory. As the old hit song by the Chambers Brothers said, 'Time has come today, won't come another day.' And as I say LIVE the DREAM DEFERRED!

Inner Journey:

☐ Reflect on your self-concept at 20, 30, 40:
What were your fears, insecurities, and
questions?

☐ What was your dream of the future; home,
work, relationships, and emotions.

Action Steps:

☐ Select and write a paragraph describing
an old dream to revive or if you have
none, create one. Do one thing to act on
that vision.

Chapter 2
Get Thee behind Me Satan

It is common sense to take a method and try it. If it fails, admit it frankly and try another. But above all, try something.   —Franklin D. Roosevelt

Courage, like fear, is a habit. The more you do it, the more you do it, and this habit—of stepping up, of taking action—more than anything else, will move you in a different direction.   —Tony Robbins

Sitting and staring at the unknown; a new blank canvas or new city or new house, I get vertigo. My usually sure balance is shaky, as I reach for a foothold to push off from. The transition to what is usually called retirement has brought up huge insecurities in me around change. The changes may be big, like choosing a new career or moving to a new city. Or low risk such as publishing my poetry and even just building a new patio in the backyard. There is a field of industrial psychology called 'work-life balance.' In retirement it might be called life-dream balance. Where were these emotional landmines hiding before the 'retirement?' In my former employment there was always a rush to get to the job, to get the work done, to promote or at least protect one's career, now I felt great relief. For awhile. Then after a few months and many margaritas and a wild road trip, in the quiet moments a new anxiety emerged. Many challenges became apparent;

physical aging, social connections, moving to the 'dream' house, and the biggie—'meaning of life.'

The above have many facets, but the one I am concerned about at the moment is the one they don't talk about in retirement planning; **fear of failure** in this new life. This time of life brings many big changes—retire from work, empty nest, body changes, and more free time. My last shift this significant happened forty years ago—graduating college and going to work. I doggedly pursued a personal/spiritual growth path over these years. Fearlessly trying new meditation practices, going on retreats and seminars, making new relationships, traveling in foreign countries, taking new jobs, my mantra was check it: And still is.

While in the cocoon of employment, I had a secure home base and jumped into the new experiences without much thought or consideration. But without the back-up confidence from the career, fear of failure in the big things loomed large. Among other things the goal of moving to a new town immobilized me, a plan to publish my book stalled, and travel to a long-dreamed of tropical idyll languished.

Fear of this type is not about physical survival. It was about the survival of my old lifestyle. As I transitioned from my old identity defined by my job, and into one largely shaped by my choices—a new rainbow of interests, activities and friends. I hit the wall. I used to run marathons, and a common experience is running fine for 15, 19, 20 miles and then the 'Wall.' The body shuts down to about one cylinder, barely moving. The crowd cheers and encourages and somehow you limp across the finish line. Pulling the trigger is tough. Pep talks and life coaches and friends and support groups can only point in the direction. They cannot take that leap into the new, the unknown, the exciting, the growing, and the satisfying.

Finally, I took the big leap and had my first solo painting show. As the event approached lots of fear and doubt arose. What if people make snide comments? What if no one shows up? To comfort myself, I wrote a bio and realized that I had something to share that I valued. Buoyed by that inner truth, I went to the opening and enjoyed it immensely. Strangely enough, some of the paintings that I did not think were good received big praise.

What caused this inhibition? Old baggage of past mistakes or failures caught up with me. Impervious to rational analysis, I carried a psychic ball and chain. Escaping from this load demanded attention. My old story was polluting the future. My old ideas inhibited taking challenges. What is the real base line fear? I analyzed the incidents that did not work out the way I hoped, then I set out to avoid or chisel those big boulders blocking my road to reinvention.

Taking the leap into the new, I called for suspension of that ancient history. I chose to be curious and embrace the change in its totality. Sometimes it looks like I cannot afford to waste time by failing now. But then I remember life is only now—this moment and then the next. One experience leads to the next. My current strategy:

1. Decide what I want to do
2. Share my vision with a trusted friend
3. Consider what is the worst that could happen
4. Evaluate the fear
5. Take the next step
6. Engage with the experience
7. Celebrate

Hello, fear of failure. Today I am taking that next step and publishing my poems and shouting out—*Get thee behind me, Satan.*

Inner Journey:

☐ Close your eyes and imagine an activity where you are afraid of failing.

☐ Share your fears with a trustworthy friend who believes in you.

Action Steps:

☐ Make a provisional plan with specific goals and next steps.

☐ Give yourself some kind of reward when you take action.

Chapter 3
No Tie, New Self:
Review, Release & Reinvention

All changes, even the most longed for, have their melancholy, for what we leave behind us is a part of ourselves; we must die to one life before we can enter into another.   —Anatole France

It takes courage to grow up to turn out to be who you really are.   —e.e. cummings

A pile of a couple hundred ties lay strewn about a table in my bedroom. I moved them when I painted the closet where they hung for over a decade. Collected over thirty years of professional employment, I treasured my ties. At work they symbolized my professional attitude. Although not required to wear a tie in my former job, I chose to wear a tie virtually every day, even as the work culture became more casual and ties became less and less common. It shaped my self-concept.

The tie completed the uniform of my job. When I put on a tie, I was preparing for work. Almost all are silk with various dramatic patterns, from cubist renderings of Picasso paintings to psychedelic musings by Jerry Garcia to red, white, and blue for American holidays and even one made of aluminum shaped like a zydeco washboard. Ties expressed my individuality and style.

I always wore the Casablanca tie on Valentine's Day, the snowman around Christmas, and the red-white and blue on Memorial Day. When it was hot, I would wear the cotton batik from Bali. Without excep-tion, I made sure the tie of the day matched my pants and jacket. Looking good was never sacrificed for my occasional sartorial eccentricities.

Soon after my retirement I went with my new girlfriend to the Los Angeles/Ventura County line beach and made a bonfire of work shoes and a stack of ties. Intent on ritualizing the change in my life, I thought the transition would be quick and easy. It wasn't. I couldn't deal with this closet of ties even after that night at the beach. They just hung there, limp, purposeless, like a collection of clothes in the Smithsonian. I was reluctant to place them back on their proper hangers. What for? I rarely wear a tie these days. The burning was a ritual closure of that phase of my life. I don't intend to return there.

We all have remnants of past personae hanging around our homes and lives: gifts from a past lover that we never use or perhaps sports gear from an earlier obsession now past. How do we handle these relics? Do we allow them to use up space in the house and mind? Do we dispose of them? Toss them out unceremoniously following the biblical admonition, 'let the dead bury the dead?' Many people pack them away in a storage bin or attic because they just can't bear to part with the memory attached to the thing.

The end of the year is often used as a time to release old stuff to create physical and psychic space for the new. I use the days be-tween the winter solstice and January 1 as days of reckoning with the year just past; make that long promised phone call, send that email to a friend that faded away, maybe write a note to myself, acknowledging the successes and failures of the past year. The tradition of making resolutions or intentions is a powerful way to begin a new year. While I am at it, I purge the closets of detritus. The ties won't go back in the closet, just as I won't go back to the old job. It is time for them to hang somewhere else: *Review, Release, and Reinvent*.

Inner Journey:

☐ Reflect on the last big transition you went through: retirement, divorce, moving. Did you ritualize the moment?

☐ Do you hold on to things, people, or places beyond their expiration date?

Action Steps:

☐ Go through your closets for unused clothes, dated paperwork, or stuff no longer useful. Reflect on that time and then toss it or give it away.

☐ Any people in your life that you no longer see but you miss? Call them just to say hello.

Chapter 4
Name Your Destiny

To dare is to lose one's footing temporarily. To not dare is to lose yourself. —Soren Kirkegaard

To change one's life: 1. Start immediately. 2. Do it flamboyantly. 3. No exceptions.
—William James

Chocolate Iguana, 212, Novel, Little Sprouts, Winning, Laughing Buddha, Jungle, and Dominican Joe's all have something in common: the names announce their mission or style. All of the above are local coffee shops each with a distinctive vibe and environment. In my ongoing exploration of non-corporate coffee shops, I have often been struck how a name can evoke a certain experience.

Some of them are highly descriptive and original, and the place is reflective of that. A bland name tends to indicate an ordinary experience. At the *Chocolate Iguana* (Tucson), in addition to coffee drinks and wi-fi, they specialize in candies and cater to a high school clientele. The *Novel* (Ocean Park, CA) started in a hundred year old room with books lining the walls. The *212* (Ocean Park, CA) refers to the street addresses and is highly local. The *Jungle* (San Diego) is outside with a bamboo décor. *Dominican Joe's* (Austin, TX) has a connection with Dominican Republic coffee. None of these is bland. Each name describes a soulful and original ambience.

On the other hand, check these names; *Sip Expresso, Café Medici,* and *Bisbee Coffee.* They don't say much and their interior designs are all interchangeable. You could switch out chairs and tables in each of them and everything would look like it belonged. Creativity, originality, and sense of place are missing in these places. If the name is plain, the ambience usually is too. Names are important. Along the road of life most people all collect various names or labels. Perhaps they are called job titles (dean of students) or roles we play (dad, mom, sis) or signify academic or spiritual achievements (Dr. or Dalai Lama). When we leave the full-time career or the kids move out of the house or we move to a new town, a grand opportunity arises— renewal, rebirth, and reinvention. A chance to start fresh.

Invent anything, and then it must be named. There is an old metaphysical maxim: **Name it and you can claim it.** For those who are interested in renewal or as AARP's initiative calls it *re*-**Imagining**, it can jump-start a new beginning. In the Bible it says, 'a people without vision shall perish.' Renowned spiritual teacher Rev. Michael Beckwith created the **Vision Process** for developing a personal dream. Having a vision sets the tone and direction of this potentially great time of life. Of course, this time can also be the long slow slide to boredom and irrelevance. It takes rigor of the heart, soul, and mind to activate this new or reborn self.

A first step may be to rename or rebrand oneself, like the coffee shops who outfit their decor in keeping with their name. A zen koan (unsolvable riddle) says: *Who would you be if you didn't know your name and story?*

Craving reinvention, I wondered, 'Where do I start?'—A favorite animal? A place? A personal hero from history? Some people go to a psychic or guru to get a new name. Erhard (creator of est/ Landmark) found his in a magazine on a plane flight back in the 70s. I took on a new sobriquet, Rhino, after a men's weekend workshop, and it fits, an animal with a tough exterior, known to charge at malefactors, and highly sensitive. I claim that name. Now, on to the next action step.

Inner Journey:

☐ Reflect on your nicknames as a teenager. Were they evocative of a quality you possessed?

☐ Consider nicknames of famous people that became synonymous with them, for example, Magic Johnson, Dizzy Gillespie, and so on.

Action Steps:

☐ Look for a new nickname. If nothing comes, then consider someone you look up to for inspiration. Use it!

Chapter 5
Someday is Here:
Dust Off Your Dreams

Seize the time!
—Bobby Seale

Catch your dreams before they slip away.
—Mick Jagger/Keith Richards

At a recent celebration of life memorial service, I saw friends from ten, fifteen, twenty years ago. One person after another got up to share memories of the departed. Relatives, lovers, close friends, acquaintances each shared a slice of the story. The sharing ranged from a couple words of love and tears to a prepared thousand word text. Of course, funerals are often old home week. Awareness of the finality of life is inescapable in this setting, whereas most of the time we ignore it, hide from it, and deny it. It is a coping mechanism that allows us to get on with 'the pursuit of happiness.' The experience got me thinking about time and us Boomers and the old Rolling Stones song, *Time Is on Our Side.* It was *then*, but not now.

We've all heard the catch phrases about aging, 'you're only as old as you think', 'I think of myself as young', 'Somday I'm gonna.'

As unspoken partner to our cultural denial and fear of death, our culture denies aging as if there is something wrong with it and acts as if death is a mistake. But we know aging and dying is inevitable. But it's not all bad news. Recognizing and confronting aging can be liberating. When I cast the discerning eye of truth to the situation, I usually see a sign flashing, **If not now, when?**

Another small reminder of the passage of time: Attending a late-night concert by an old music hero from the 70s, Dan Hicks, I sniffed a hint of marijuana in this 55+ crowd just like back in the day. I felt 21 again, until I left the concert suffering from lower back pain—never had that forty years ago.

Admitting our years is not popular with my peers. It is a sad and somber topic for a generation who virtually made a religion of youth. Remember 'don't trust anyone over thirty?' I visited a friend from high school and he said he doesn't feel older. Usually, I don't either til I look in the mirror or get up in the morning. How do we reconcile the inner self-concept with the external reality? Is it necessary? Can one live in two worlds, feeling young and being 'older?' I like that idea, but a scary thought arises: Imagine you are dying soon and you realize that you missed important stuff, because you thought you were still young and had plenty of time?

Staying fixated on the illusion of perpetual youth can prevent one from doing what is really important. We've all thought it, 'Someday I'd like to . . .' A recent survey of individuals on their death-beds yielded insights into what is really important. The interviewees knew there was not much time left and all they could do was look back with bare honesty. Some of their regrets we've heard before; *I would have spent less time at the office or I would have kept up with old friends.* The comments were not surprising but, they exposed deep feelings. The one that hit me the hardest was the proverbial bucket list. *I haven't done things I always wanted to do.*

Lately, dusting off old dreams has been a practice of mine. For example, when I was thirty I had a dream to play in a reggae band on a tropical island. But I put that idea on the back shelf in a mental box called *Someday*. I buckled down to a practical life with a professional career and got the 'gold watch.' Pulling the old plan off the back shelf and checking it out was a wakeup call. My lifelong dream was no longer viable or appealing.

I share this story with people in their 20s and 30s. *Do it now or make tangible plans to do it*. If you wait til much later, usually the person who had that dream has changed, or the world has changed. At my manifestation group the other day, a woman in her 30s said she wants to live in France for a year. She made it happen this year.

For us who have now reached the next chapter of life, check out those bucket list items. What still has juice? What can you do with joy and enthusiasm? Then make a plan and take the next action step. I wrote this essay on a tropical beach in Mexico, where half the population is North Americans of all ages, who are living their dream of a winter home in the tropics. The others? Lobster-red, snowbirds. Breaking out of the home routine, exposed me to a range of people making different choices.

In Mexico, I met individuals in the Boomer age bracket who are riding motorcycles overland from Canada through Mexico, others living in a trailer for the winter and practicing violin, and many who manage a business from here. They are living a dream, not waiting. I wonder how my life would have been different, if I had not waited for *Someday*. But not for long, it is time to dust off that *Bucket List* and take action . . . **Today**.

Inner Journey:

☐ Remember age 20-25. What did you want to do? See? Produce?

☐ If you didn't even try, what got in the way? Keep it real.

Action Steps:

☐ Make a five-item Bucket List. Make sure they are things that are largely within your power to do.

☐ Make a plan and take the first action step for one of those items. If you fail, dust yourself off and get back on it.

Chapter 6

Catching the Wave in the Last Third

It is never too late to be who you might have been.
—George Leonard

Wholly unprepared people embark on the second half
of life...but we cannot live the afternoon of life according
to the programme of life's morning—for what was great
in the morning will be little at evening, and what in the
morning was true will at evening become a lie.
—CJ Jung

This year attending the conference was easy. I didn't have to fly across the country, but simply got on the Santa Monica Freeway and drove downtown to the L.A. Convention Center. Either way, it was a chance to meet a far-flung tribe and I learn:

How to document the stories of my life

- techniques of repacking my life
- the value of having an empathetic ear in relationships
- the importance of following the unknown path before me
- how many steps and how many calories it takes to explore a convention

And that was sandwiched in between;

- joy of free shopping bags, water bottles, ear plugs
- the excitement of driving a fast race car

- uninhibited and joyful exercise of zumba
- synergy of playing in a drum circle
- wisdom and insights of a well-educated ,intelligent all-time great NBA star
- and the power of thousands of Boomers who aren't done yet

Where did I find such a cacophony of experiences? AARP's 50+: *Life Reimagined* annual convention: Defying the mockery of my friends, I attend the national convention every year. How come? I am a dreamer AND a realist. The bottom line is that aging is inevitable and often it is challenging. Change is inexorable and sneaks up on you. One day you are 45 and everything works well, settled on a career, happy in your relationship, comfortable in finances, and immersed in avocations that you've nurtured for years. Then turning the corner of 60, plus or minus a year or two things change.

You may retire from your career voluntarily or not, a newly discovered body part causes aches and pain in the morning or after a sport, or an intimate relationship with kids or spouse mutates. For me, suddenly I woke up and realized I was not in my 40s any-more. The thoughts and feelings may be sudden or subtle but it was unmistakable: I was older.

What did I do then? Similar to the grief process; 1) *Denial*: I am not old, I can do everything I used to, I have plenty of time, 2) *Anger*: This is not supposed to happen, I'm still young, 3) *Bargaining/Compensating*: OK, I'll get cosmetic surgery, buy a Porsche, and take naps, 4) *Depression:* I'll just stay home and watch TV and surf the internet and maybe return to the drugs of my youth, 5) *Acceptance:* I am this age with all of its changes/challenges and hopefully wiser and I'll do the best I can with work arounds (yoga instead of running marathons). And my add-on from Martin Seligman 6) *Flourishing*: Live with joy, purpose, vigor, and passion. The crowd I mostly saw at the convention lives that way.

They are older persons who confidently claim a place at the table of life in a society that marginalizes, insults, and denies aging. We are in an era of active aging where 60 is **not** the new 40, but a totally new stage of life---active, purposeful, creative and contributing. I watched conventioneers collect info and freebies. Not content to stay at home and isolate, these people came to grow and to connect with each other and the flow of life.

When I attended the annual convention, I felt connected to possibilities and inspired to wake up and live. I embraced elder hood and at the same time felt great humility to be given this time to reinvent, renew, and revive. I met fellow explorers who ranged from fresh faced 55-year-olds to octogenarians in motor-ized carts, some in shorts and velcro shoes and others in long gray dreadlocks and ethnic prints. At a music vendor, I saw an impromptu dancer who could've been on stage, with her looks and shape and fine moves. Contrary to the media-induced popular image of older people, the AARP crowd is engaged, vigorous, passionate, and life affirming. They are practitioners of AARP's initiative—*Reimagining*. And in that world you don't want to lay back on the easy chair and wallow in nostalgia.

Inner Journey:

☐ Have you come to grips with aging? What adjustments have you made?

☐ List 10 activities or experiences you would like to do that are completely new for you.

Action Steps:

☐ Find a group for one of those new things and attend at least a few meetings or class.

Chapter 7
Pursuing Zorba's Secret

I get up. I walk. I fall down. Meanwhile, I keep dancing.
—Rabbi Hillel

Action is the antidote to despair.
—Joan Baez

All the problems we find so complicated or insoluble he cut
through as if with a sword . . . it is difficult for him to miss,
because his two feet are held firmly planted on the ground
by the weight of his whole body.
—Kazantsakis
from Zorba the Greek

My home office looks like a used bookstore that specializes in self-improvement, spiritual, and philosophical books. It has been a passion for thirty years. While preparing for a recent trip, I decided to break this habit. The programs, theories, and con-cepts of my books and all the workshops had blended into the labyrinth of the Minotaur who could not escape. Wanting to read about a life well-lived and fully expressed, I decided on *Zorba the Greek* by Nikos Kazantzakis, appropriately set on the same island as the Minotaur, Crete. There wasn't time to order it from Amazon, as I was about to leave for a trip. Checking my public library and several used bookstores, inquiries to literary friends were all futile. Caving to the chain store, I went to Barnes and Noble. Upon handing my $25 gift certificate to the cashier, I got a strange response. "Sir, our lines are down for gift cards.

I can only take cash or credit." Frustrated, I declined to buy it and walked out.

But he did not even look round. How could he possibly have talked at that moment to a bookworm who, instead of wielding a pick, held in his hand a miserable stump of pencil? He was busy. He did not wish to speak. ("Zorba the Greek")

On the way to the car, it hit me: I am done reading about life. Life is to be lived right now in the present, like Zorba. No more reading about Zorbas but living like Zorba, with zest, vitality, energy, purpose, passion, and *in the body*. My self-improvement zeitgeist had become a solipsistic merry-go-round. Round and round and round. Being a good student and a graduate of a career in public education, I always believed the answers were in books and classes. Study was my obsession, not living. Finally tired of preparation, I wanted to just do it. For the recent retiree it may be even more poignant, since the sands in the hourglass are running out.

About a week later on my trip to the East Coast, I chanced upon a used bookstore in Salem, MA. Hidden in between shops selling witch costumes and broomsticks, it was the most crowded bookstore I'd ever seen. The proprietor only had a ten-inch space to peer out. I asked for *Zorba the Greek*. He said "Sure. Right away." He picked it out of one of the 10-foot tall stacks. I immediately began devouring it, despite my vow to not read.

In Zorba, Kazantzakis (a Christian mystic) explores life's meaning in ideas and characters. I saw myself in the protagonist. Like me, he is a writer and a student of life—in books. He encounters Zorba, who is a working man who lives full-out; dancing, singing, making love, fighting wars, and traveling to many countries. But Zorba is not simply a hedonist, he is also a thoughtful man and ponders questions such as the meaning of life. But his solution is not reading, but dancing to get the answers. Drawn to this totally different and liberated soul, the narrator realizes he must stop living in his head and allow the soul and body to lead.

Inspired by the book, I now wanted to see the 1964 movie. It, too, proved elusive. I mentioned my interest to a friend and he called to tell me that it would be on TV on a certain day. I planned to record it, but then forgot. Thinking that a vintage, classic movie would not be hard to find, I put in a hold request at the library. I waited for several weeks and the tracking report said it was in transit, meaning that it was turned in and on its way to my branch. After another week or so, I went in to the library and inquired and they reported that it had been in transit for six months and was obviously lost. Giving up on that outlet, I dropped into my local indie video rental store. They looked it up, 'Nope, checked out.'

Surprised but into the hunt, I went home and joined Netflix streaming because I really wanted to see the movie immediately. Turned out it is not available on streaming, only on DVD. I put the idea on the back burner. The next day, stuffing the mailbox was a notice from my public library, 'Sorry we couldn't get the DVD, but we will do an inter-library loan for free.' Yet again, I was unable to procure the Greek ode to living.

Finally I ordered it from Netflix and viewed the film immediately. Cloaked in the patina of a black and white, the film portrays the key events from the novel, but not the inner quest. Although the performance by Anthony Quinn was nominated for an Oscar, the film barely scratches the surface of Kazantzakis' spiritual inquiry. Zorba comes off as a wild, free, unattached man who chases his passions, without the inner reflection the narrator explores in the book.

That is what a real man is like, I thought, envying Zorba's sorrow. A man with warm blood and solid bones, who lets real tears run down hs cheeks when he is suffemg and when hes happy he does not spoil the freshness of his joy by running it through the fine sieve of metaphysics. (Zorba the Greek)

My quest for this book and movie demonstrated to me that living fully can be studied in a movie or a book but doesn't replace action. I find it especially relevant these days when virtual experiences are considered normal. People walk down a beautiful street looking at their screens. Zorba says, 'Look up and see what is obvious.' Some things can't be answered with an Internet search. Sometimes we have to pull a Zorba---dance, sing, and play music. Stop study and analysis, and muster the courage to live life. And *act*.

Inner Journey:

☐ Consider a goal that you have researched, planned but not acted on. What holds you back? What is at risk?

☐ Visualize achieving that goal. How does it feel? And what if you failed? Is it worth it?

Action Steps:

☐ Make a plan and take the first step for that goal. And then do it again, if that is a miss. Do it at least three times before quitting.

☐ Reward yourself for the effort and/or the success.

'You Can Check Out but You Can Never Leave'
—The Eagles (Henley, Frey, & Felder)

PART 2.
PLANNING AND STRUCTURE

Chapter 8
Close Kitchen Doors and Unleash Your Power

When one door is closed, many more is opened.
—Bob Marley

If you must begin then go all the way, because if you begin and quit, the unfinished business you have left behind begins to haunt you all the time.
—Chogyam Trungpa Rinpoche

Ever walk through your kitchen closing, cupboard doors and drawers? Maybe you're like me and go around shutting the open lockers in the locker room at the gym. Why do we close them? Perhaps, they'll get in the way as we walk through and slow down our progress. In addition, before I leave the house I also make sure everything is in its normal place. Then I feel ready to go out.

Unfortunately, it is not so easy to close doors in our head. Back before I 'retired,' most of my open projects were managed by the circumstances of the job. Things needed to get done, and a timeline was imposed. I was always on the go; making lists and checking things off even in my off time. There is a natural momentum in a highly scheduled lifestyle. After quitting the job, the focus went from 'what do I *have* to do' to 'what do I *want* to do?' From external locus of control to inner.

One of the little advertised facts of retirement is that many individuals who go from employee to retiree fail in that transition. Either they (more often men) get depressed and die quickly, or get bored and return to work. Surveys indicate that most of these returnees to work do so to feel useful and productive. That is not a bad thing. But I think if the return to work is not due to financial necessity or a burning passion, it is a default solution to an existential question—what's my life about?

For many, retirement allows the time to pursue long-held goals and dreams. A website has compiled the world's most common goals and in the top fifty nothing is even vaguely like *relaxing*. But to achieve personal goals, it takes the powerful skills that entrepreneurs practice: *Self motivation and management*. As an employee I had a built-in system that organized my time. Without the job structure to produce results, I find it easy to start projects, then get distracted—no boss, no deadline.

Unfinished projects don't go away—they linger in the background of our minds, like ghosts haunting us. Sometimes depression appears and then the thought arises that work is more rewarding than retirement, so back on the hamster wheel. Don't rat yourself out. Identify incomplete projects or goals or dreams, whether it's planting an organic garden in the backyard or starting that online business or taking a class in origami.

One day, when feeling a gnawing unease I was given noted productivity guru David Allen's *Getting Things Done.* In spite of my self-talk that I didn›t have to be productive, a lightbulb went off in my head and I began to conceive of this stage of life, retirement from the daily 40+ hour grind, as a project. And it consisted of many sub-projects. It is not a vacation and therefore deserves the attention and planning that I gave to my career in education

Allen considers all aspects of life a project. He encourages individuals to get control of all of the projects in their lives from maintaining the house, to keeping fit, to career advancement, to child-rearing.

Like many people, I had many goals that I wanted to pursue when I had the proverbial 'free time.' It wasn't like flipping a switch. Some projects I wrote down as vision statements but after awhile I noticed how many of these ideas seemed to stall. In surveying my projects and bucket lists, I noticed what Allen calls 'open loops.' Closed loops have a beginning and end and are complete. Unfinished projects, or open loops leak energy and clutter the mind. I looked at the projects in my life, from planning a trip to remodeling the house, to getting the car tuned up, to learning badminton. After I identified the open loops, it got real simple and powerful, 'What is the next action step?' Do it, close the loop, and move on! If it isplanning a trip, then the next step might be looking up flights to the intended destination. If it is repairing the house, call the contractor for an estimate. And so on.

The main thing is to stay with the concrete and not the abstract. When we think about postponed projects, they are either big and complicated, vague and mysterious, or even just tedious. The perceived difficulty can stop us before even starting, and we end up with a lot potential projects. Is that so bad? Not necessarily, but in that case Allen recommends a Maybe/Someday folder for those goals we are not yet committed to. Moving a project into the action folder, says I want to get this done—soon.

I gathered up those goals, projects, and tasks and listed each one from 'auto repair,' to 'Zambia trip.' In the collection, process I ended up deleting what turned out to be ideas, not projects, and fantasies, not dreams. Anything remaining was assigned an action step. One longstanding project was remodeling the front of my house. Therefore, the next action was to call the contractor. Immediately after calling him, I felt energized. By taking action, I felt more life. Studies show that minor successes can create as much endorphin rush as major ones. Nowadays, I find open loops, take action steps, and bask in the positive vibes of being my own boss.

Inner Journey:

☐ List the projects you have started that are still incomplete. Decide whether each one is still desirable and, if not, put it in Someday/ Maybe list.

☐ Identify the next step for each live project and give it a due date.

Action Steps:

☐ Prioritize the tasks to be done and do them.

☐ Give yourself a reward (pat on the back) for closing loops.

Chapter 9
Got To Build Your Life on a Strong Foundation

It's time. If you are to walk the path of heart, then it is time . . . —*Nippaawanock*

Often the unconscious will solve a mystery that the intellect has struggled with in vain. —*Carl Jung*

Gazing at my newly 'demoed' backyard, my thoughts wandered to another non-professional builder who worked in his backyard. For decades, Carl Gustav Jung repaired to his stone tower on the shores of Lake Zurich at his home in Bollingen, Switzerland. There he painted mystical images, speculated on ancient rituals, and wrote books. Jung was a man of towering intellect, who along with his former mentor, Freud, dominated 20th-century psychology. He largely built the tower with his own hands. On many of the stones of the tower he inscribed symbols from ancient myths. Begun in 1922 upon the death of his mother and regularly added to until the death of his wife in 1955, he believed that physical activity released the unconscious and yielded insights into the forces that influence personality. Throughout his life he studied the world's mystical traditions and their applications in the modern world. Mystic, thinker, and scientist, he bridged Eastern and Western philosophy.

Re-landscaping my backyard got me thinking about Jung building his tower and how it applies to my reinvention after 'retiring.' My journey of individuation from my former career and lifestyle has taken many unexpected twists and turns. Before quitting, I expected to implement my lifelong dream of moving to a tropical island. Right on time, I met and fell in love with a Jamaican woman. It felt ordained. We made plans to move to Jamaica, Hawaii, or . . . ? She seemed to fit right into my house in Santa Monica with its tropical rattan furniture and artifacts from countries between the Tropics of Cancer and Capricorn. Sadly, the tropical dream was too much for a relationship that had a weak foundation. After much *sturm und drung,* it crashed.

When our relationship imploded, I discovered extreme wood rot in my backyard deck. It needed replacing, and I demolished the deck, board by board. After a long marinating period with the yard a wasteland, I finally had a vision of how to replace it. I bought the materials and another long delay ensued. Finally, over a year after the first rotten board was pulled, I went to work in the yard and began installing the stones. I did not think of Jung, but I was also working in stone. Placing the flagstone of my region (just as Jung used granite quarried in the Alps), became a practice of meditation, expression, and manifestation. I felt I was building a new yard/patio AND my life. I found freedom in my backyard, power in moving the stones, and creativity in my daily work. Reinvention was no longer an abstrac-tion but a real thing. Observable, tactile, and original, I was now living a new life both inner and outer.

My yard demonstrated a widely cited theory of motivation and personality developed by Edward L. Deci and Richard M. Ryan— *Self Determination Theory*—which postulates that *autonomy* (doing it independently), *competence* (effective results), *relatedness* (connecting with others) are corner-stones of happiness. They believe that motivation does not require all three but must satisfy at least two of the three elements. In this case, I had the first two.

This was the first time I had done such work. But as I lay each stone, faced a dilemma, and solved it, I experienced satisfaction. My new life was manifesting. Building a strong container (be it friends, community, career, love) takes careful attention and patience, but first you clean the hard drive, debug, and *then* install the new programs, to mix metaphors. The three little pigs were right all along, you've got to build your life on a strong foundation. And I can walk on mine.

Inner Journey:

☐ Consider a time when you jumped into something without doing the necessary preparation.

☐ Think about some of your current plans or goals. Are they really yours?

Action Steps:

☐ Identify a personal goal. What competencies will you need to learn?

☐ Sign up for a class and/or enroll a confederate for support.

Chapter 10
Savor the Flavor, Then Take Step One

What is important is to keep learning, to enjoy challenge, and to tolerate ambiguity. In the end there are no certain answers. —Matina Horner

Only in quiet waters do things mirror themselves undistorted. Only in a quiet mind is there a more complete perception of the world. —Hans Margolius

A few days ago I attended a local meditation group for the first time in a few months. In this circle there is a round of updating and sharing around topics where individuals are facing a growth edge or a challenge. I spoke about living in L.A. and where I stand right now with that and other areas of my life. A couple days later one of the members said I seemed clear, calm, and grounded. At the time, I did not feel any different, but that reflection highlighted an inner shift that has been brewing for awhile.

It felt like a sweet spot of acceptance of my life and at the same time, clarity about the trajectory of my plans. Taking the time to imbibe the nectar of this time since retiring yielded an unintended benefit: patience and acceptance. My career pattern for twenty-seven years was to learn the skills of a particular job and within a few years move on to a new one and begin the process again. Never one to rest on my laurels, I had an undercurrent of nervous energy that kept me moving, looking for fresh work opportunities and success. *The grass was always greener*.

After I exhausted the school district job options, I retired. I was in a hurry to get on with my long nurtured dream of living on a tropical island. Soon I discovered that renewing my life meant rebuilding virtually from scratch. My thirty-year-old dream had major fissures that needed rehabbing, reconstructing, and reviving. And that doesn't happen overnight. Retiring is one of life's most significant transitions and as such is a process that can take years.

My backyard turned out to be a metaphor for this major lifestyle reconstruction. I inspected the old, rotted backyard deck that needed replacing and estimated about a month's work. The project turned out to have its own timetable and it took over two years. It had its own schedule and taught me to slow down. Each phase of the project evolved after calm reflection. At one point I stared at the empty yard for several months. Not confident in my masonry abilities, I hesitated tackling the tough part—installation. Finally I began and momentum and confidence grew. Eventually, I experienced the gratification of successful learning and productivity.

We Boomers have a large backlog of experiences to draw on for encouragement *or* discouragement. Novelty is inherently interesting. Starting, trying, and succeeding at new experiences satisfies. But as we age, oftentimes there is a default thought that says, 'can't do that' or 'I'm too old.' Especially when it is something difficult, like my backyard project. A renowned expert on procrastination, Tim Pychl, says the trick is not just Do It, but just begin.

If I proceed without reflection and awareness, I'll probably have a backlog of undone, half-completed plans cluttering up my emotional AND physical space. Another example, in my fourth year at UC Berkeley I was in a hurry to graduate and like a lot of kids wanted to get on with my life. It seemed like every day was a year and time was wasting. Although I did not have a plan for after graduation, I just wanted to get out. I finished a quarter early and returned to my hometown and then got busy spinning my wheels jumping from one thing to the next. My immediate post-graduate period was a watershed and set a tone for much of my life. That decision to move home still carries some regret. The college experience is something I did not sufficiently savor and since retiring have made regular visits to Berkeley to link my past to the present.

Now, in another transitional time (retirement), I have allowed big changes to move at their own, organic pace. Leaning into the questions and not grabbing for quick, ephemeral answers. As the renowned meditation teacher, Osho once said, 'Don't just do something, sit there.' After the calming of turbulent waters, life then bubbles up naturally, without the maelstrom of second thoughts, fears, choices, and the unknown. So, now I savor the flavor of the moment and then take the first step.

Inner Journey:

☐ Reflect on your life and remember a time that you were in a hurry to finish something; school, a job, a relationship, a creative project.

☐ Think about a project that is pending— What kind of skills are needed?

Action Steps:

☐ Take action— buy materials, study how-to, and plan.

☐ Spend a few minutes acknowledging yourself in writing.

Chapter 11
Even Wild Animals Don't Like Cages

When patterns are broken, new worlds emerge.
—Tuli Kupferberg

To contact the truth of whom we are, we must engage in some activity or practice that questions what we assume to be true about ourselves.   *—H. Almas*

The day was long as it approached the Summer Solstice. Hanging on a patio, I spied a desert tortoise coming out from his hibernation. Like that tortoise, I had awakened and meditated on my own hibernations and/or distractions. Sometimes they are necessary activities, such as cleaning the house or washing clothes that must be done. But other tasks are pure diversion; a web search on the eleven children of Bob Marley, a conversation with a passing neighbor, or even a trip to Trader Joe's.

Such activities may be pleasant but are they the highest and best use of my time? Aligned with my purpose? Is it fun? Is it 'busy work'? A typical response from most people when they are asked how they are is 'keeping busy.' Is busy its own reward? It certainly was not in prehistoric times. 'Skylarking' (Jamaican slang) or taking it easy was a major part of the day. They communed with others and nature—time to be more mindful of life—slowing down and allowing the dust to settle. I am discovering that much of my life is busyness: Activity with no or little value added.

Musing on my freedom from the 9–5, from a draining relationship, 'self-improvement' seminars, and rental properties, I faced a big void in the area of 'have tos.' I had much more free time and the question arose? What are my true core needs? What goals come out of those needs? Drilling down to that deep self was not easy. It called for much reflection and meditation after which hopefully clarity of purpose emerged. Then the challenge was to maintain focus and to avoid distractions and busyness that robbed time. Blocks also appeared in unconscious avoidance habits—such as taking two hours to read email or reorganizing one's desk. Many of us spend large amounts of our time in activities that are 'not important and not urgent' in Stephen Covey's terms.

Getting a handle on where we actually spend our precious time is crucial for living a fulfilling life. I examined my activities with the assistance of a form created by Joe Robinson, author of *Don't Miss Your Life*. It revealed how little of my time I actually spend on what I say I value.

The self study showed that I spend lot of time on email and internet searches and more than I thought on driving around town. A two-mile trip to Trader Joe's can easily eat up a couple hours. Answering the day's email often consumes another two. This is especially relevant for new retirees. After leaving structured careers and jobs, they suddenly have 50–60 hours per week to fill. The external controls are off, and it becomes important to develop internal structures that support new goals and purposes. This free time allows for a new balance of meaningful and pleasurable activities.

So what? The patterns, habits, routines of life define what your life is about. I used to spend 60 hours per week on the job and the remainder of the time on maintaining my life. My life revolved around work. Then I realized that life is short and each day is more valuable than the gold I can earn. Recognizing that time is a resource just as money is, I looked at my weekly routine.

Once I gathered the data (in education we call that **assessment**), I reflected on what is important to me? Is it going out five nights per week for entertainment and then recovering from the night-before excesses most of the next morning? Is it driving in traffic to run an errand? How about long-winded chit-chat with friends and family? Reading today's paper? Unconscious routines or structures may make me feel secure but don't always fulfill, like empty calories with no nutrition.

After awareness, comes support. Since most of my day is almost habitual, I looked at breaking some habits. Some I kept because they provided benefits. Others have to be broken or at least done after the important things are handled. Support from other keeps me focused when it is too easy to slip into routine with no pay-off.

I enroll other people to keep me accountable to what I say I want to do. Nowadays, I have regular meetings with friends on two different topics of primary interest for me. In those meetings we take notes on Google Docs and thereby hold each other to our agreements by writing down what we said and promised to do. At one point, I and a friend started a support group—*Creative Collabora-tive Cagebreakers*—for breaking through the unconscious bar-riers and real barriers that keep us stuck in our artistic lives. We have an eclectic mix of personalities who help each other see blind spots that have us spinning our wheels.

Living for today and yet not wasting the precious time I have left is crucial. We may have thirty or forty years of active life in front of us, so I strive to make it fun, rewarding, and a service. As Bob Marley said, 'Emancipate yourself from mental slavery. None but ourselves can free our minds.'

Inner Journey:

☐ If you find you're not achieving goals or are overly busy, keep track of your time for a week. Then compile it and decide what you can eliminate or reduce.

Action Steps:

☐ If you tend to ward distraction, set up a schedule and post it on a white board, so you can see it every day.

☐ Check off your efforts each day.

Chapter 12
Break Free but Be Sure to Have Guard Rails

Trust your hunches. They're usually based on facts filed away just below the conscious level.
                                        —*Dr. Joyce Brothers*

If you don't know where you are headed, any road will take you there.   —*George Harrison*

After a one-hour side trip off the interstate, I eagerly anticipated the promised big views on the eight-mile scenic loop in Chiricuahua National Monument, AZ. Somewhat surprised to see only a couple cars in the lot at the visitor's center, I noticed a man sitting on his bumper and quaffing a beer in the noon-day sun. No alcohol prohibited rules here. After getting a map for reconnaissance, I inquired about the scenic loop. "Sorry" the ranger said, "It is shut down to replace the guard rails which were burned out in the big fire in May." That thought ricocheted through my inner experience of this road trip. *You can drive around, but without guard rails (structures) you are in danger.*

Living in the Los Angeles megalopolis my whole life, I have always enjoyed the peace and open space of the road. On this long solo trip, I experienced something very different. The formerly comforting open road became a confrontation with my insecurities. The unstructured format of my trip with no fixed itinerary or appointments, worked on my mental state like the road without the guard rails. I drove around but my peace of mind was at risk.

Boundaries, commitments, and schedules were absent and all I had was a vague notion to drive to the East Coast for the first time in my adult life. I planned to rely on my inner guidance for direction. That strategy was intentional because I wanted to trust my intuition and the synchronicities that arose. I did NOT account for the value of a PFD (personal flotation device). I have often laughed at the mandated PFD for scuba diving or boating, because I am an excellent swimmer. On the road trip, I figured that my inner guidance eliminated the need of a PFD (personal flotation device) or back-up plan for the trip.

Strengthening my inner trust was one of my covert goals, while the overt goal was to meet and interview individuals across the country who had reinvented a new lifestyle or career. Unaccounted in this scheme was my deep need for structure. The result was excessive preoccupation with the basics; where to go, when, and whom to interview. I discovered without appointments, activities, and assignments, the bogeymen (doubt) would come a knocking. Like the guardrail at Chiricuahua (which is probably rarely bumped, but serves to provide security and comfort for the driver), a daily barrage of all kinds of decisions became the prominent discourse in my thoughts. With the neurotic in charge, there was no room for the *Creative* to visit. Coming from a highly structured work environment, after retire-ment I found the greatest joy is to be without schedule. It **felt** liberating to enjoy that freedom but denying the value of struc-ture backfired. As career oriented employees we get used to routines, schedules, and chains of command, especially men (the root word for patriarchy is the same as pattern). The human brain is designed to seek and make patterns in life. So when a major pattern is excised at retirement, often disorientation emerges. Then we get to experiment with equilibrium of structure and openness. The need for that balance was the biggest take away of my ***driveabout.*** My journey to the American outback without plan, destination, or schedule did not achieve a primary goal—to reach New York.

My trip with no script showed me my freedom's edge and how to work with it. The lack of guardrails at Chiricahua did not prevent me from seeing the spectacular mountain island with its tall minaret like spires formed by erosion. I hiked a couple miles into the canyon and basked in the great view without the buzz of cars coming into and out of pull-outs. I totally enjoyed the place and recommend it when traveling between Tucson and New Mexico. But I do wish I had seen the eight-mile scenic drive, complete with guard rails. And on my next road trip I made an itinerary and plan (in pencil), then checked to see the road is open.

Inner Journey:

☐ Imagine yourself dropped into a strange foreign city. You don't know the language, and you don't have a guidebook. How do you feel? Anxious, excited, curious, lonely.

☐ Remember a trip that was highly scheduled. What is the most prominent memory other than the postcard image? Is it a side street you took? Someone you met?

Action Steps:

☐ Take a drive out of town with no destination other than traveling north or east etc. What did you discover?

☐ Do some research on that place. Did you miss something?

Chapter 13

Everything is Provisional: Make Your Plans in Pencil

He that binds to himself to a joy, does the winged life destroy; But he that kisses the joy as it flies,
Lives in eternity's sunrise.   —*William Blake*

I learn by going where I have to go.
                    —*Theodore Roethke*

Millions of dollars are made by promising that you can have anything you want. Adherents of these teachings are often refugees from religions that seem stifling with dogmas such as good people get 'pie in the sky by and by' and bad people suffer weeping and wailing and gnashing of teeth down below. Some promulgators of New Age culture also promise 'pie,' but this pie you can eat right here on earth—pretty seductive. But I think we are better served to live authentically right here and now with all of its glory and the muck and the mire. Reality! What a concept.

No book, no comfort food, no drug, and no person can really help or fix me because there is no solution. It's called **life**. But around the world most people pursue lasting happiness and sometimes call it god. This obvious insight arose during an altered state. It came up while I was driving north on I-5 through the summer oven of the Central Valley of California. As a 110-degree furnace blasted my face, and the sound system served up the trance music of Fela Kuti, my analytic mind rested. I had escaped from the deepest nadir of my post-job life.

To many, it may appear that I've got it made and that has been said to me many, many times. (When I hear it, I cringe inside and give myself ten emotional lashings—'What is your problem? You're health is excellent, your house near the beach in Santa Monica is paid for, you're financially secure, and most importantly your time is your own.') But that day when I looked in the mirror, abject hopelessness looked back. Several people around me were experiencing emotional duress and had reached out to me for help. I absorbed as much of their karma as I could, and then hit the Wall.

Maxed-out on emptiness, no schedule, and vague goals, and although patient to a fault, I could absorb no more. After clearing my schedule, the Animals circa 1965 called me, '*We Gotta Get Outta This Place.*' My comfortable home and neighborhood were a whirlpool sucking me down. Like kayaking when you hit an eddy, I knew that the only way out was backwards. In this case backwards was to a place I knew well, where the waters were calm.

Restoration waited at my favorite hot springs resort in Northern Cal. There I would immerse myself in the healing waters and escape from places and activities that played in an endless loop-the coffee lounge where I write, the personal growth groups I attend, the jazz clubs I frequent, the gym I go to 5x per week, and the never-ending traffic jams I drive in. Out of that vortex and in the open space of mountains and hot springs, I could reconnoiter. In the waters nestled between the mountains I'd rejoin my community of fellow voyagers of the soul and spirit.

Upon arriving at Berkeley for the night, hopelessness returned. I lost the clarity and insight that the straight line of I-5 encouraged. But somehow my forty-year love of reggae music got me out of my motel and to an outdoor reggae festival in the Oakland hills. Walking into the amphitheater and hearing familiar melodies of Third World, a huge smile crossed my face. I was home among a crowd of strangers in a strange place, a community that bonded through a common passion. Another mood shift.

Originally, I planned to figure out what I needed to do to start my engine again. My answer book of the moment was *A Unified Theory of Happiness by Andrea Polard*—a great book. Full of useful info and exercises, but I forgot it at home. Thank god, I realized it was a crutch to avoid diving into the real feelings and experi-ences. I surrendered to what was—a week of reflection at the hot springs. Polard calls it the Supreme Mode—harmony with the universe.

Before it happened, I idealized retirement as a life free of schedules, plans, and order: spontaneous free expression. Barreling down that long, hot freeway something shifted: I embraced the value of both pure beingness and planning. Even when plans change, they provide the structure to live life positively, not aimlessly. When I just float in the waters of life and let it take me where ever, I am tossed and tumbled every which way. But breaking out of that eddy and guiding my vessel on the river of life, has been tough. The job imposed structure and goals on my life and without it I tend to drift.

Following the white line at 80 mph, it hit me—goals are not written in stone but are provisional. And they have a place. Goals got me to Berkeley and the concert, to the waters of Harbin, and the light in my soul today. But they can and do change.

After soaking for a week, I set a course for my drive home. Naturally, it was modified—ah, true freedom. It was a great trip, with order and surprises. When I got back, I parked the car, unloaded the stuff, and returned to my life, a little older, a little calmer, and ready to engage this provisional world again with a plan and goals **in pencil.**

Inner Journey:

☐ Consider a time when you were depressed or stuck and didn't know what to do. How did things shift?

☐ Do you live without clear plans and goals?

Action Steps:

☐ Go counter to your usual style. If you plan trips in detail, go someplace without a reservation, plans, or goals. If you tend to take off without anything more than a destination, plan it complete with reservations, activities, and goals.

☐ Take a long drive in the country and keep a pad of paper or recorder near you. As new ideas and dreams arise, write them down.

'Just Can't Wait to Get on the Road Again'
—Willie Nelson

PART 3.
DISCOVERY AND ADVENTURE

Chapter 14

Apocalypse Now to The Way: Adventure Awaits

We don't know all the reasons that propel us on a spiritual journey, but somehow our life compels us to go.
                    —Jack Kornfield

The only question in life is whether or not you are going to answer a hearty 'yes' to your adventure.
                    —Joseph Campbell

Ever have the experience of let-down when you finally visit a famous landmark? That sense of 'is that all there is to it?' That reaction is perhaps becoming more common these days as we get bombarded by communication, both visual and aural, just about every place. Freshness is hard to come by. Adventure and novelty stimulate our minds and spirits. Consider the first time you visited a famous place, the memories you have are usually about the people you meet or the weather or the local culture. Famous locations have been embedded in our minds for so long that often the actual experience is less exciting than the surrounding experience.

On the other hand, after a long trip, I experience joy returning home to the comforts and routine of my life. It feels good to reenter the known and secure world of home. Finding that sweet spot of novelty balanced with comfort can be a challenge. It can be especially daunting for Boomers after years of experiences as we move into the mature years. The contrast between youth and maturity is illustrated in two classic Martin Sheen movies, *Apocalpyse Now* and *The Way*.

In each film, Sheen plays a man who is charting his own course. In *Apocalpyse Now* (1976), set in the Vietnam War, Sheen plays Willard who is assigned by the brass to go up the river to take out Colonel Kurtz (Marlon Brando). In this interpretation of Joseph Conrad's novel *Heart of Darkness*, Willard faces all manner of madness set in the midst of the Vietnam War. He goes upriver where tribal loyalties carry more weight than any government. Kurtz has gone rogue and Willard's mission is to terminate him. They have a meeting of minds and Willard senses the hopelessness that prompted Kurtz's descent into the shadow. Although he understands and we suspect sympathizes with the reasons for Kurtz going off, Willard kills Kurtz. He returns to the command and it is implied that the road has been paved for his successful military career. But underlying his compliance with orders, Martin Sheen's encounter with freedom, madness, and the unknown clearly changed his character's world view.

Fast forward to 2011's *The Way,* produced and directed by Sheen's son, Emilio Estevez. Again we see Sheen in the role of a conventional man, an ophthalmologist in Santa Barbara, CA who has a call to destiny that changes his life. His 20 something son (played by Estevez) leaves graduate school to see the world and begins the pilgrimage of St. James in northern Spain. On the first day of his two month hike, the son is killed and Sheen decides to take his place. After that decision, his life changes irrevocably.

In both films Sheen is summoned to pursue the unknown through no wish or will of his own. On both journeys he faces unimaginable foes, characters, situations, and inner turmoil. In the earlier film, his reflections are prompted by the external evil of the Vietnam War and a renegade US Army officer, while in the more recent movie the loss of his son provokes an inner jour-ney into the darkness of the soul, but the characters around him are largely benign. In *Apocalypse Now* one imagines that even though Sheen goes on to success in his career and a conventional life, he is forever changed and tormented by his experience into the heart of darkness. In *The Way*, Sheen's character picks up his son's backpack and on the trail confronts his grief. The film ends with him turning his back on the comfortable life and opting for the unknown and adventure.

As bookends of a typical life, both films illustrate the transition of moving into retirement for the countercultural Boomers. For many, formative years were spent in rebellion, creative expres-sion, freedom-seeking, and community. Then, on cue, most of us settled down (like Willard) into careers, mortgages, children, and routine life. The chaos of our youth is symbolized by the horror of going up the river to take out Kurtz. Then much of our generation traded materialism for rebellion in the '80s and '90s.

That phase fades for many of us somewhere around age 60. Now, we can thrust wide open the doors to freedom and heed the call of the unknown. The new adventure is not the horror of Vietnam, but the excitement found on a new road—*The Way*.

At this stage of life, many don't have to stay on the roundabout of life circling to work and back, broken only by an annual two-week vacation. The opportunity is there for recapturing the spirit of youth tempered with the wisdom, hopefully, of age. We may rediscover curiosity and discovery and leave behind the ersatz Paris/Venice/New York of Las Vegas and explore the real world. When I travel, first I visit the tourist landmarks and then i poke around the nooks and crannies of the side streets away from the monuments. Adventure is found in the unknown places, both inner and outer.

Inner Journey:

☐ Write about a traumatic experience of your past. What did you learn from it?

☐ Think about an emotionally risky adventure you took. How did it turn out?

Action Steps:

☐ Visit that place or person and do a ritual of closure. If that is not possible, then find a photo; say a prayer and give thanks for the lessons, and burn the photo

☐ Identify a place in your area that you have always wanted to visit. Go there, and write about your discoveries.

Chapter 15
Pre Dawn Urban Safari

Where a man's edge is located is less important than whether or not he is actually living his edge in truth, rather than being lazy or deluded.   —David Deida

Action may not always bring happiness; but there is no happiness without action.   —Benjamin Disraeli

There was a chill in the air, as we walked to the local artists' café in the pre-dawn dark. My co-conspirator and fellow writer, Ravendove, and I had made a pact to open a new creative window and then see what escaped. At 4 am, the café was very quiet one older guy drawing with colored pencils and a group of four chatty young people pulling an 'all nighter.' Finding a table was easy, not like during the day when the place is filled with single individuals and their laptops. At this hour a vibe of mystery lay heavy, with 70s funk music in the background. Our plan was to look at the *same old, same old* with new eyes—hoping to see new and different stories without the overlay of habit and pat-tern in this very familiar place.

We sure did see different stories; the guy doing an intense calis-thenic workout on the boardwalk, the homeless sleeping on the beach fifty yards apart, the go-getter vendors staking their place on the boardwalk, the bleary eyed kid bumming a cigarette, and the locked restrooms. After sunrise, the people of the night slowly faded away and a new crew appeared; a young couple on their morning walk, the backpacking kids outside the coffee house, the street performer with his bulging muscles glistening in oil, and the salt of the earth waiting for their bus to work.

This experiment alerted me to the need to change setting and/or set to stimulate reinvention. Long familiar with the refreshment and renewal that comes with travel to unusual places with no fixed agenda, I consciously forged a crack in the routine reality of my home neighborhood. Same setting with a different mind-set, the mind-set of the middle of the night. Through that sliver emerged a 'new' place, new characters, with new energy.

As we age, most people become habituated in thoughts, habits, and emotions. This default development may lead to a stifling ennui. I've used the novelty and excitement of traveling to store energy, for when I return to the mundane routines of life at home. That experience is not only available out of town but right where we dwell. The challenge of reinvention and revival requires a new mental set. Thinking isn't enough, it takes action.

Sometimes I get bogged down in 'been there, done that' mind-set, but the pre-dawn safari awakened my taste for potential new passions. After the midnight safari, I felt ready to tackle that long submerged plan to learn guitar, to take up badminton, and to write the next chapter in the book. The middle of the night trek transformed the familiar setting into an exotic locale. I saw new people, different shops, and cultural variety all on a two-mile walk from my home.

This netherworld of the graveyard shift stimulated me without invasive searches found at the airport, without the back stiffness of a long car drive, and without the hangover of overindulging in my drug of choice. Renewed and re-calibrated, I was back on an efficient and effective path for exploring and developing new passions and *living the dream deferred*.

Inner Journey:

☐ Write a few sentences about what happens in your neighborhood in the middle of the night. If you don't know, imagine.

☐ Reflect on adventurous activities you have never done and what it would feel like to do them.

Action Steps:

☐ Get up in the middle of the night and go some place familiar.

☐ Go to a completely new place at any time of the day and spend a couple hours.

Chapter 16

The Exploration Benefit: Here, There, and Everywhere

I learn by going where I have to go.
—Theodore Roethke

Without change, something sleeps inside us, and seldom awakens. The sleeper must awaken.
—Frank Herbert

Meet me in El Segundo? El Segundo! I know where it is, but why would I go there? Suggested by a very hip and culturally astute poet friend, I was intrigued. Although I had lived in the L.A. megalopolis my whole life, I had never been there. But seizing the hint, I said yes. Located a half-hour south of my home in Venice, just past Los Angeles International airport, El Segundo is a small city of about 15,000. These days Angelenos tend to carve out areas of activity due to the numbing traffic. Certain areas, perhaps no more than 10 miles away, can have such an aura of distance that it feels like you need a passport to go there.

I broke the mold this day, turned left, turned left again and suddenly I was off the freeway and in Middle America, sampling the local vibe. Main St, El Segundo is about three blocks long, with the high school at one end and the city hall at the other. In between on the pedestrian friendly street are a variety of local shops from cleaners to beer bar to yoga studio. I passed two other non-chain cafes before settling on the *Blue Butterfly Coffee Lounge*. It has sidewalk seating and comfortable couches inside. I expected good food, because a couple of police sat down next to me. My spirits had lifted in the ten-mile drive as much as a four hour flight to Hawaii. Something new and at the same time comfortable and easy.

A local vacation like that is available to virtually anyone almost immediately. Escape from routine, banality, and into novelty stimulates good feelings. This hard-wired human trait, known by anthropologists as the *exploration benefit*, developed when we were hunter-gatherers because visiting new places improved chances for survival. For modern humans, when we dip into the stimulation of the new, the unknown, the mysterious, the happi-ness hormone dopamine flows.

Finding our personal balance of the known and comfortable in life and the new and challenging requires experimentation. Visiting a new place in your hometown doesn't have to be saved for out-of-town visitors who want to see the big sights. It can be as simple as walking down a new street or driving to work on city streets rather than the freeway. When something catches my eye, I stop, look, and linger.

One of my passions is visiting non-corporate coffee houses. That's where I find the local ambience. Each offers common features, such as a neighborhood bulletin board that helps to make me feel at home, and their own distinct features, such as a performance stage or kid's play area. I have a favorite locals' coffee house in Honolulu in the Kaimuki district called *Coffee Talk*. When I stop there, I can instantly settle down to work without disorientation. Last time I visited the barista gave me a kama'aina (locals) discount. If I happen to be on the North Shore, it is the same vibe at the *Coffee Gallery* in Haleiwa. They have a lanai (patio) section for computer workers. It is so relaxed that one man posts there every day and interviews tax clients. Home away from home, discovered by getting off the main travel arteries.

Maybe you love spas. I do. Virtually every neighborhood has a spa these days. It is easy to walk around a new neighborhood and get a facial. Put feet on the ground and experience life as it unfolds. Our two-ton traveling homes (cars) can act as a barrier between us and new places. Connecting with a place is connecting with its life. Drive to a new area, get out, and explore. Too much of the same old, same old deadens.

Sometimes I need a kick start to activate my novelty gene, like the case of my friend suggesting El Segundo. It wasn't on my screen, never thought of visiting that town but when the idea arose I said YES. Instant energizer and cure for the boredom blues. So, I keep my eyes and ears open for ideas and invitations to break into a travel adventure right here at home. I find a destination that feeds an interest or passion and park the car and walk. Quickly it is discovery time and ennui disappears. Pretty soon I am foraging in the wilderness like a caveman and that is exciting.

Inner Journey:

☐ Make a list of nearby towns (within one hour) that you haven't visited. Pick a couple and research for interesting sights.

Action Steps:

☐ Go to one of those towns and *stop, look, and linger.*

Chapter 17
Pursuit of Passion (Hot Springs) Leads to Adventure

I have accepted fear as a part of life, specifically the fear of change, the fear of the unknown. I have gone ahead despite the pounding in the heart that says: Turn back, turn back; you'll die if you venture too far.
                                        —Erica Jong

It takes practice to hear your true desires. Your passion will often come as a whisper or serendipitous event that reminds you of what's important and what makes you happy.   —Eckhart Tolle

One of my lifelong passions—hot springs (from luxury spa to hot water bubbling in a make-shift pool) has re-energized. My all-time favorites include the steam bath/pool in the lava flow on the big island of Hawaii as well as the chic, full service spa at Glen Ivy in Corona, CA. Pursuing this avocation leads me to unexpected adventures and discoveries.

Driving an unpaved road in my Volvo subcompact for an hour in Southwest TX epitomized my devotion to hot springs. The siren call of healing waters inspired this long side trip. In fact, the call of hot springs was the theme of my three-week *driveabout* around Southwest USA. From the recently upgraded *Ojo Caliente* (near Santa Fe, NM) to Truth or Consequences, NM (formerly named Hot Springs) to *Eldorado* (outside of Phoenix), each has its own particular style, mood, and reward. And in each place the camaraderie of the hot springers prevails.

Chinanti Hot Springs, at the end of that unpaved road, highlighted this spirit—a classic scene where the soakers bantered about the relative merits of hot springs from Big Bend, TX to Wasilla, AK. They ranged from pensioners spending the season in their RVs to day trippers from the nearby city to international travelers on a world tour.

But getting there was more than half the story. Fueled by memories of past hot springs, located in natural settings, soothed by the mineral waters, and mostly by my sense of adventure, I headed south from Marfa, TX and opted for the shorter (by half) unpaved route. Bad choice, but based on my many years of travel to war zones, nature outposts, and the Mojave Desert, how bad could it be? A lot worse than I thought. Just before the paved section ran out, I spied a Border Patrol truck pointing in the direction of Mexico. I recalled a recent news report on how smugglers are prone to bring their human cargo overland from Mexico through the Sonoran desert here.

Initially, the unpaved section was well-graded and easy to drive but eventually narrowed into a single lane, ungraded, winding mountain road. Picking my way through the large rocks and steep climbs, the 405 freeway at 5 pm suddenly seemed speedy. I had to stop at dry creek beds to move rocks out of the way, all the while praying to not have a breakdown of some sort. Or even worse meet one of those smuggling crews who would have nothing to lose by commandeering my vehicle. My imagination was hard at work conjuring up disasters and I had no cell service. Passing rusting ruins of old vehicles did not lighten my mood. After about an hour without seeing another car, an old truck approached from the other direction. I wanted to stop and tell my story, but the old guy just waved and kept rolling. After hitting the paved road at a village called Ruidosa, I felt like an old-time cowboy riding into a frontier town. But there was no saloon or even convenience store, just a boarded up church. Deflated I trudged on for another half hour on more funky roads.

When I finally reached *Chinanti Hot Springs* and told my tale to the proprietor, a middle-aged lady who moved there five years before, she just laughed and declared my passage to be a miracle given the condition of the road. However she added, "Even if you had broken down, Border Patrol had a blimp in the air and saw your every move." So much for isolation. After my hour's soak and kibitzing with my new hot springs comrades, I took the 'twice as far' paved route back to the Interstate. Enough adventure for one day.

Another hot springs surprise was my exploration of the strangely named Truth or Consequences, NM (or T or C to locals). Although right off the Interstate about an hour and a half south of Albuquerque, the town looks like it had been abandoned in 1955 and then rediscovered a couple years ago. Old broken-down hot springs motels litter the town. Boarded up and derelict, they look like a scene from Mad Max, but on the main street are several gentrified shops selling everything from organic vegetables to crystals to used clothes. The gem of the town is *Riverbend Motel and Hot Springs,* which has four tubs of varying temperatures overlooking the river. Recently, it was redone by the thirty something owner in a style reminiscent of the Palm Springs chic 'mid-century' look.

Santa Fe, NM yielded a wild and scenic treat. As a frequent visitor to this acclaimed and unique art town, I had previously sampled its local treasure, the city's adjacent chic spa, *10,000 Waves*. Enticed by friends' recommendations for *Ojo Caliente Mineral Springs,* I drove an hour north of the city. A shower of yellow-leaved cottonwood trees greeted me upon leaving the highway at funky Espanola—notable mostly for its cheap gas. Mile after mile of the yellow-leaved road was a visual delight comparable to the fall leaves in New England. At Ojo Caliente, I discovered hot springs that offered a stew of different mineral baths, arsenic, lithium, sulfur, lead AND a separate mud bath. Each mineral said to be curative for things such as psoriasis, rheumatism, arthritis, and so on. Like a frog, I jumped from pool to pool.

On the final leg of the road trip from Tucson, AZ back home to L.A., my hot springs passion led to the obscure *El Dorado Hot Springs* in Tonopah, about an hour west of Phoenix. Beat up heavy construction vehicles decorate the front yard. As you enter the compound (walled in with wild bamboo), an electronic alarm goes off. Walking into the yard reminded me of visiting an Old West movie set, wood-frame buildings, an old trailer, and an outdoor office set up on a table. I asked the toothless proprietor about a collection of rocks and broken bottles on the folding table. She reported that it is just stuff they pick up in the yard. On one side of the dusty yard are the semi-private tubs, and at the entrance a sign announces, 'Warning You Are Entering Nude Area.' A collection of five old claw-foot tubs and one converted aluminum water tank comprise the baths. No juice bar, massage, or changing room. Just take off your clothes and jump into a homemade, trailer park, style hot springs resort.

Passions lead me to unknown places in myself and the world. It pulls me into situations my analytic mind rejects. My passion for hot springs pushed me off the fast route, the interstate, and into surprises. Beautiful vistas, friendly people, scary roads, strange architectures, healing waters, and a variety of sublime moments were my reward. Find a passion, let loose, and PURSUE IT. Don't let your fearful, comfort-seeking mind take your eyes off the prize. The reward is the experience, and the experience cannot be televised, tweeted, or Skyped.

Inner Journey:

☐ What have you failed to do because it looked dangerous?

☐ What is a passion you pursue? Do you go out of your way to do it?

Action Steps:

☐ Go some place that excites you--- music concert, or a type of city or terrain.

☐ Celebrate the place and reward yourself for the effort.

Chapter 18
Providence in Providence, RI

To my mind, the greatest reward and luxury of travel is to be able to experience everyday things as if for the first time, to be in a position in which almost nothing is taken for granted.　　　—Bill Bryson

I think the purpose of life is to be useful, to be responsible, to be honorable, to be compassionate. It is, after all, to matter: to count, to stand for something, to have made some difference that you lived at all.
　　　　　　　　—Leo Rosten

Recently, I made a side trip to Providence, RI after a buggy and difficult week on Cape Cod. It rewarded me with great discoveries. When I arrived at the state capitol of Rhode Island, shock— several free parking spots greeted me. Ready for the $4 per hour that is standard in downtown L.A., I was pleased to find an hour remaining on the meter AND the rate was only $.75 per hour. In the tradition of state capitols, an armed guard and a massive, ornate cupola awaited inside. No crowds, no wait, this side trip was easy.

There to handle some family business at government offices in Providence, I had a mission. Not mission impossible but a mission easy, as it turned out. After meandering lost through the halls and legislative chamber, I requested directions from a fiftyish bored state police. More than amiable, he directed me to another building behind the capitol building.

Steeled for a long wait with a cache of reading material, I pulled a number and the clerk appeared. I blinked to make sure I wasn't at the Apple store or some other customer-oriented vendor. Friendly and agreeable, she took ample time to explain what I needed to fill out. I asked how many days to get them. "You can wait. I'll have it in fifteen minutes." I needed coins for the meter, and a helpful customer at the cashier offered to give me as many quarters as I wanted. The clerk gave me the docu-ments and directed me to the next office about one mile across town.

At the secretary of state's office a similar scene played out, but even easier. Two clerks jumped to serve me, did my *apostille* (even though a handout said it would take two days). They encouraged me to handle the last piece of my document recovery mission and printed a map to direct me to the office. Driving through downtown proved a challenge to my usually perfect sense of direction. But getting lost on the winding, one-way streets turned out to be a pleasant tour of a renewed city.

Throughout the new Providence, you'll find ancient (by California standards) buildings perfectly restored. It is an easy walk from the government buildings to the shopping mall to the riverside park to the downtown arts district and the financial district. Everything is within a few blocks.

Allowing my intuition to guide me to the state archives office, I drove straight to it and found another parking spot with time on the meter right in front. The state archives guy gave me a slip of paper to fill out, which also warned of a two day delay. He took my info and went directly to the files and returned with my document.

By this time in my odyssey of state offices, I was on a cloud. This state works. Everything flowed smoothly. How do they do it?— Especially with downtown parking at 75 cents per hour. Starting with my easy time at the Blue State Coffee near Brown University through the parade of state offices, everything flowed effortlessly. But that was just the warm-up for the main act, Federal Hill. My cousin in Boston warned me that the old Italian neighborhood was not what it used to be. He said that it had been taken over by hipsters, I feared the worst: a phony imitation of a traditional ethnic enclave and subsumed in too hipness, like downtown LA and most gentrified places.

Having arranged to meet another cousin for dinner, I took Atwell St to Federal Hill. Cruising the commercial street, I looked for De Pasquale Piazza, the heart of Italian Providence. All along Atwell are homey restaurants with a few tables outside to take advantage of the summer weather. Another easy park (no meter, no valet), and I ambled to La Dolce Vita Cafe' on the square. Passing several groups of old Italian gents gossiping, I hit the square and was faced with another surprise—It oozed authentic-ity. Five or six outdoor restaurants and a big fountain filled the piazza. One restaurant offered customers to select a live chicken for their dinner.

My cousin, Belinda asked: "How was your mission in Providence today?" I said, "I can't believe how much fun and easy this mission was." We caught up on family stories and gorged ourselves on real Italian food—*che bella*. Then the dulcet sounds of an ersatz Frank Sinatra waffled through the air. A young man in a black suit and tie serenaded the whole piazza in the sultry summer night.

That day in Providence, showed me that cities can have grace and ease. The renaissance of Providence began during the long mayorship of Buddy Cianci (the first Italian-American mayor), who sparked the transformation of a city that was considered at the time to be a pit. Now, its light shimmers and is worthy of its name—redemption. Indeed, it was providence for this soul, who has wandered in some inhospitable regions. After a stint in the pen, Cianci went on to sell a highly successful line of pasta sauce. And is now taking another run for mayor (2014).

I dug it—a worthy mission, a fresh location and a wild ride. I had clarity of purpose, got in the flow, and let providence (trust of life) take over and had a great time. And perhaps like this Boomer, who is sometimes afflicted with 'been there, done that,' you can check out an old haunt, whether city, beach, island, or country. Like Providence, founded in 1636 by Roger Williams, who proclaimed it a haven, it may have had an extreme makeover.

Inner Journey:

☐ Do you have a mission that requires a visit to another place? It could be a quest or anything that takes you to a place you wouldn't go for vacation.

☐ Then, think of places you have visited that did not live up to their promotion.

Action Steps:

☐ Go on that mission with no expectations.

☐ On item two, do some advance research and see if there are any new attractions or positive changes.

Chapter 19
Everything Is Not on the Internet

For those that have eyes let them see. For those that have ears let them hear. —The Bible

How can you follow the course of your life, if you do not let it flow? —Lao-Tzu

Don't look too far ahead or you'll get overwhelmed. Just do the next apparent thing. Keep putting one foot in front of the other. —BJ Gallagher

On my way up to Harbin Hot Springs (Middletown, CA) for my annual retreat, I decided to change the routine a bit this time. Instead of my usual 8, hour bullet drive in one day from Santa Monica, I stopped in Oakland to visit with an old college chum. I planned to take a leisurely drive to the hot springs about two hours north of the Bay Area. In preparation for this trip I had searched the Internet for some interesting night life jazz, reggae, or spoken word in the East Bay. After all, these days everything worth doing is online, or so I thought—I found nothing. No worries. I let go and surrendered to whatever happened in the moment.

The flow took me to Jack London Square in Oakland, CA to meet my friend. Located on the old waterfront or Embarcadero, for many years it was a seedy and blighted area. Then major redevelopment hit in 2000. Now it is an upscale, mixed use development---condos, high-end restaurants, bars, and hotels. But in the nooks and crannies of this sterile world are surprises.

We met at a 'casual' restaurant on the square named *Haven,* which has utstanding seafood. But that is not the story. Walking to the restaurant, next to the new yacht harbor, I saw a log cabin. Odd for a new redevelopment with five story buildings surrounding an antiseptic walkway around the marina and ferry berth. A few feet from the log cabin were maybe fifty young professional types drinking in a man-made patio of decomposed granite, sand and heat lamps. They had spilled over from the bar (the *First and Last Chance Saloon*, circa 1883), which has been there so long that its floor is three feet below the current street level. You have to step down into it to order a drink, and inside it slopes catawampus. Very cool and real deal place. Local writing legend Jack London spent many hours there sipping his spirits and writing. The bar is the sole remnant of the old seedy waterfront, not a replica but a true survivor.

And the log cabin? The Klondike Hut is authentic, well, actually, half real. It was found in Alaska, where Jack London wrote some of his famous books. They shipped half to Dawson City, Canada and half to Oakland and then reconstructed it true to the original drawings.

That was not the end of the 'not on the Internet' treats. Walking around the new waterfront, we found a super cool bar with a four piece jazz/salsa/pop band. I must have had a jazz vibe, because the next morning in Berkeley, looking for a cool spot to check my email and have breakfast, I went to Telegraph. It felt like desolation row with several new empty lots and boarded up windows and no people. I passed and went to another excellent spot on San Pablo Ave, but they had a line out the door. By chance I came to the 4th St shopping area and had a coffee. Posters indicated that on Sunday the street was closed for a free jazz festival.

Another non-internet surprise occurred at the *Oakland Museum of California*. Drawn by an exhibit of political protest posters of the sixties and seventies, my Berkeley radical days came to mind. As is my wont being a writer, I pulled out my pen. "You may not have a pen out," admonished a voice from behind me. I looked around and saw a twenty-something young woman in a guard's uniform. Stunned, I inquired about the reason and in the flat tones of bureaucratese she responded, "You could damage the post-ers." Need I say more about this glaring irony? Moving on, I shook my head and thought, 'thank god for the Patriot Act.' The museum is safe from dangerous pen wielders. Bet that rule is not men-tioned on the museum's website.

What did this mean to me? Make enough plans to get your ship to sea, but don't presume or prejudge what you'll find there (think Columbus). A common idea these days is that everything can be found with an Internet search. None of the above pleasant surprises were found online. I tried. I looked. But in vivos, on the ground, stuff arises that can't be planned. Like the last person you fell in love with, it happens when you least expect it. Another reminder, now with the ubiquity of the Internet, we think we know where we are going, but I keep my eyes and heart open and pleasant surprises sometimes appear. I ask myself--- Are you ready? Are you open to see or do you have blinders on? Do you listen to your gut or your head? Then I plan and get ready for surprises.

Inner Journey:

☐ Recall the surprises on your last trip out of town. Were they positive? Negative? What were the conditions that allowed them to happen?

☐ Take a few minutes to plan a trip in your head, accounting for most of each day.

Action Steps:

☐ Plan a day trip and do it. Make sure to do something off the plan. It may mean taking a side road or visiting an unexpected museum.

☐ Spend an hour doing things without thinking or analyzing your decision. For example, if the idea to go to your car arises—just do that.

Chapter 20

Taking that Detour May Lead to Freedom and Home

Clinging to the banks of the river may seem safe and more secure, but life's possibilities are truly engaged only when we trust, release and become part of the flow of the universe.   —*Chelle Thompson*

When I let go of what I am, I become what I might be. When I let go of what I have, I receive what I need.
                            —*Tao Te Ching*

Getting off Interstate 40 and driving the straight, flat, state highway to Bisbee, AZ, I felt like a city interloper in my compact Volvo passing farmers in big Ford pickup trucks and their one street villages. Not oblivious to the cultural changes in urban areas, one of the villages had its own nail salon/yoga studio. But it was country. Pursuing my goal of discovering the *creative* soul of America, I had a tip that Bisbee was an art town grown over an old mining town. Little did I expect an outpost from Occupy Wall St. populated with Venice Beach-style bohemians within a stone's throw of the Mexican border in the Sonoran Desert.

The *Welcome to Historic Bisbee* sign glared from the strikingly beautiful and ugly at the same time open-pit copper quarry, once the most productive in the US. Taking a photo, I reflected on the hidden beauty of our earth which was revealed by strip mining. The aggressive pursuit of ore revealed multicolored striations of red, green, and purple rock.

This road trip was initiated to explore the authentic smaller art towns of the US by trusting word of mouth and intuition. Although I used a guidebook, as an experienced traveler I know that the spirit of a place often varies widely from what is written about it. The guidebooks report a quaint old mining town with artistic flavor. Steeling myself for a tacky and soulless makeover of an original town (Prescott, AZ style which is notable for shiny Indian war statues and chic restaurants in the former brothel), I had just passed on Silver City, NM due to time considerations. I couldn't allow myself to bypass on another possibility. In this case, I wasn't compelled by passion but fealty to my purpose.

I rolled into the town and parked. The place reeked of uniqueness. A couple of young men in long hair and beards rolled by and smiled. I wondered, 'how did they get here?' Walking around, I saw a house whose front was a bouillabaisse of bizarre statues, colorful paintings, and 'found art' junk. Another one was painted red and white stripes. Across the street an artist was painting the scene. Then I came to a vacant lot that would have fit well at Burning Man. Old concrete retaining walls were painted in various colors and streamers and paintings flew in the breeze. On the second level overlooking the street, a motley collection of tents surveyed the scene. Signage indicated alliance with the Occupy Wall Street movement, then current.

Later, in conversation with an older guy in long, gray hair whose last home was a boat in the Bahamas and a young man in his twenties who works two nights per week at a restaurant, I learned the story. Bisbee has been inhabited for years by a cohort of free spirits sometimes called artists, sometimes hippies but always refugees from mainstream culture. Now, with the OWS movement they have taken over two lots in the center of town. Both men were friendly and welcoming in the spirit of this authentically 'quirky' town. In fact, my new acquaintances said that many people in the town are paid by their families back home to stay there. In addition to the arty funk, several old hotels have been rehabbed but not 'gentrified.' Every building exudes originality.

Bisbee is real, from its dirt paths connecting uphill to street level, to the drainage pit with a sign that threatens death if you go in it, to the early 1900's Queen's Mine Hotel and its front yard of rusting mining equipment. The only new building in town is the misnamed Convention Center, which is really a collection of tour-ist shops. The harmonious mix of the old mining town, the artists, the busy-at-noon bars, the chic old hotels, and the natural setting excited my eccentric nature. Just how I like it, creativity, antiquity, all ages, and sunny skies.

As I usually do in places like this, I asked the older guy from the sailboat how he got here. He said he was staying in Scottsdale, AZ with its cookie-cutter housing tracts and franchise-only shop-ping centers, when his brother said, "You belong in Bisbee. Be off with you." I then queried the young man serving the free food, he answered "word of mouth." Then he asked, "Are you looking for a home?" His question pierced my heart, like an arrow. Was my yearning that obvious? They had what I craved, community, authenticity, and creativity.

Driving out of town, I reflected on the importance of taking that road less traveled. The road that leads to the soul's fulfillment. Whatever path I take, I strive to trust my head *and* my intuition. Sometimes it is a side road through the flatlands and fields that may lead to home. And if not a home, a view of another lifestyle.

Inner Journey:

☐ As usual, reflect on a time you got off the beaten path willingly. What happened?

☐ Imagine being on a tour of a place that you have never visited before. Then, think about taking a half-day off while the group goes to the scheduled stop. What would you do?

Action Steps:

☐ Take a day trip to some place routine. While at that place, do something new and hopefully out of character for you. For example, get in the car and just go. Don't overanalyze.

Chapter 21
The Side Road to Miracles & Art (Marfa, TX)

It is good to have an end to journey toward, but it is the journey that matters, in the end.
—Ursula K. Le Guin

People usually fail when they are on the verge of success. So give as much care to the end as to the beginning.
—Lao Tzu

The typical reaction to a detour is frustration. The trip will take longer, the road may be rough, and probably miss certain scenery. But an intentional detour can offer the real boon of a road trip. Even in daily life in the city, as Robert Frost wrote 'the road less traveled made all the difference.' Pushing through habits, routines, and expectations offered for this rebirthing *Boomer* the excitement of discovery. A side trip to the mysterious town of Marfa, TX had my favorite elements, desert, art, classic hotels, and hot springs. Approaching from the east on I-10, the setting sun against the mountains in the distant horizon beckoned me to the unknown.

The state highway, a straight ribbon of asphalt traveled only by jumbo, six-wheel pickups and the occasional semi-cab, stretched to the horizon. I learned of Marfa from a chance acquaintance at a gym in Santa Fe. My curiosity had been piqued. But is it worth a three-hour detour? On the other hand, what could be more exciting than an art town that had no silver jewelry shops festooned with Southwest Indian dream catchers? Even the Chamber of Commerce website trumpeted its obscurity, with its most significant landmark an ersatz Prada shop done up in a derelict roadside café 38 miles outside of town and now left to the elements.

The website also listed a super chic motel (*Thunderbird Motel* with its appropriately retro hip name and minimalist style) and a classic, luxury, old downtown hotel (The *Paisano* built in 1930). I knew there must be something about the burg, when the website mentioned a set of renovated (in desert art style) casitas that are fully booked for six months. The final enticement was the revelation that this 'art town' did not even have one dive bar. Whoa! Isn't that one of the enduring stereotypes, the long suffering artist with a shot of Jim Beam on the counter?

I headed toward the Rio Grande with the cautiously open mind of an offbeat and wary traveler who had recently experienced the tsunami of bus tour shoppers at Santa Fe. As a creative type and art lover, I get bugged when a cool art town becomes a commercial hit and caters to formulaic motifs---wolves baying at the moon, angular whistle blowing kokopellis, and turquoise, big belt buckles (Santa Fe, Taos). Heeding the call, I barreled down the road into Texas cowboy country, slowed by the cowguards in the road every twenty miles or so. The first one I hit with a bang to the suspension and the next I went nice and easy.

Before arriving at Marfa I passed through Alpine, which is the proud home of Sul Pass State College, a college town with not even one coffee shop hang out. The big excitement centered on the local Dollar Store. Downtown shops were boarded up, but a brave tourist information center proudly offered free coffee and wi-fi. I picked up some fruit in anticipation of slim food choices in Marfa. That fruit saved the day on my trek out to the hot springs the following day. Just before getting into town, I noted a viewing platform on the side of this flat road.

Marfa turned out to be a special treat. It has been the location shoot for at least three Hollywood movies (*Giant*, *No Place for Old Men*, and *There Will Be Blood*). With its windblown desert ambiance, the stately county courthouse, and the regal *Paisano Hotel*, it exuded the old west. A quick stroll around town revealed vacant shops in the center of town right next to a gallery with an installation from L.A. Across from the converted gas station pizza parlor, another gallery hosts pieces in the $30k range. In a side room the gallery owner negotiated with a well-dressed, mature art investor.

The scene would fit in West Hollywood or New York City. Next to the new NPR radio station is the public library, which that evening had a screening of original animation shorts by a local filmmaker. Within a couple more blocks is the regional headquarters of the Border Patrol and their housing area with clean, rectangular, non-descript abodes. Walking back to my luxury hotel, I passed beat-up old houses with the roofs caving in next to super-chic gentrified old adobes. My favorite was a converted church. And like in a ghost town, I saw no people.

Needing a drink to assimilate this incongruity, I walked back to the hotel bar, with its older, well-dressed, and proper guests. The conversation was too erudite for my mood, so I split for a slice of organic pizza and spinach salad at the converted gas station. Overhearing a local's comments about the Marfa lights, I headed back out of town for the evening spectacle. With no bar or movie theatre, this seemed to be the only game in town

At the previously noted viewing platform, about a dozen tourists traded tall tales they had heard about the how to see the 'lights.' Since I had been prepped by the locals, I instantly saw the *light*. It appeared to be a flickering star very low on the horizon. The blurb on the newly constructed platform declares there is no scientific explanation. Scientists supposedly consider it a '**miracle**.'

Reflecting on that word miracle, on the way back to town, I realized I got more than I asked for in Marfa, an art town with vacant shops, high-end galleries, luxury hotel, too-cool motel, Border Patrol, and the Marfa Lights. I found pure gold on this side trip, unexpected, unplanned, unusual, and different. Glad I made the three-hour detour, I remembered that miracles happen when you least expect it. Like the Marfa Lights, they are better left unexplained.

Inner Journey:

☐ What is your idea of a miracle?

☐ Recall any detours you have taken?

Action Steps:

☐ Intentionally take a different route to work or some place you go to often. Make a note of what you see.

'I Believe in Miracles' (You Sexy Thing)
—Hot Chocolate (Brown & Wilson)

PART 4.
INTUITION AND
SYNCHRONICITY

Chapter 22
Ritual and Ceremony
Prime the Pump of Reinvention

What is accepted by the majority of people does not mean it is real. —*The Buddha*

We are born in mystery, we live in mystery, and we die in mystery. —*Huston Smith*

On a cliff overlooking the Pacific Ocean at Esalen—one of the original personal growth centers established in 1961—our group of twenty-five scribbled their wishes, hopes, and dreams on scraps of paper. After passing a candle and a bag of tobacco, each person burned their paper and tossed it and a pinch of tobacco into the sea. The class ended, and the group dispersed and went their separate ways. It may sound banal and quaint to the modern, scientific mind. What effect could that possibly have in mani-festing something in the 'real' world? Since college in the 70s at Berkeley, where I first encountered the *I Ching*, ritual has been an essential aspect of my life. Perhaps it is because I am a recovering Catholic with a mystical bent, but it works for me.

Many years ago, during a protracted romantic break-up, I went to Hawaii to assuage my pain. One day on the coast of Kauai, sitting on a lava rock I wrote a letter of good-bye and a prayer of well-wishing for her and myself. Burning incense, the letters, and a photo, I wallowed in my tears. When it was over, I was cooked. After returning home, the next Sunday at church I met my next girlfriend—on Valentine's Day no less. Coincidence? I had tried to end the former relationship for months, but the burning ritual marked closure (if only in my own mind and soul). It was really over and I was now open for the new. I wiped the slate clean and I sent it out to the universe.

The above ritual consisting of a pinch of tobacco, whole body smudge, a random Tarot card, a prayer written and burned, and sharing led to an unexpected career opportunity for one of the participants in the workshop. She had revealed her concerns about a professional conference in Europe and if she would be invited to attend. A couple months later, she was awarded a prestigious position at the conference. Our rational, thinking minds can't imagine how those arcane actions could impact the material world. But something shifted and stuff changed.

Much has been written on the power of attraction, pro and con. The realm of the unseen and intangible elicits high emotion from both rationalists and metaphysicians. Too often highly emotional commentary shuts out the value and truth of both positions. Rationalists say that praying and wishing for something won't make it happen. On the other hand, millions dogmatically follow the metaphysical doctrine of 'as a man (person) thinketh' and insist that that is all it takes. Staying open to the metaphysical, while grounded in the material requires samurai like balance of the sword of discernment.

Deliberative and pragmatic by nature and training, I came to esoteric teachings with a skeptic's mind. "How does it work?"

"What is the evidence?" "How do you define god/spirit?" With low tolerance for the latest fad during my career in education, I was known for asking tough questions from ivory tower presenters. They offered theories, not experience. Usually, the 'new reform-best practices' were repackaging of the same methods I experienced in school fifty years ago. 'Keep it real' is my motto. However, as the great 20th century metaphysician Ernest Holmes taught, I keep it open at the top. In other words, when something works, makes sense, and is useful, I do it.

Back to rituals and manifestations: Many of us who pursued a traditional career for thirty-plus years have a built-in wariness for fluff. After all, we have survived for decades by figuring out the program and following it. But how do you reconcile experienced based realism with irrational systems such as the *I Ching, Runes, Tarot,* and astrology that have been used for guidance and insight by millions for millennia?

Sometimes images and notions bubble up from the subconscious mind. And in that state of mind ideas and answers arise that would otherwise never have occurred to us. An experiment in Holland some years ago proved when difficult, unsolvable questions are posed to subjects before sleep, the solutions come to conscious awareness upon waking. They concluded the power of our mind is greater than our ability to access. With practice, ritual can also help us to tap that great reservoir of knowledge.

Will just affirmation and prayer get the results I want? It may happen, but as Peter Tosh said, 'Take one step toward heaven and jah (god) will find you.' One thing that distinguishes people from animals is volition. Our behaviors are more than instinct, we think and choose. When we act, we put our time, ego, and heart on the line for the goal. Priming the wheels of the unconscious with ritual and ceremony focuses power and sends a signal to the world. But active effort sparks the engine that gets the vehicle of manifestation moving.

Tools for guidance range from rituals and ceremonies to meditation and prayer to journaling. Discover and incorporate the ones that resonate with you. At the same time, follow the admonition of the early metaphysicians, 'Treat (pray, affirm) and move your feet (take action).'

Inner Journey:

☐ Consider any oracular system that you might use—Tarot, I Ching, Runes, Ouiji Board, astrololgy. What do you do with its 'advice?'

☐ Do you practice conscious ritual in your life? What is its purpose?

Action Steps:

☐ Try a new oracle and ask a question that has been vexing you and see what insights come to you. I alternate between *I Ching* and the *Tarot* to keep my perspective fresh.

Chapter 23

Don't Need a Weatherman to Know Which Way the Wind Blows

Intuition is the supra-logic that cuts out all the routine processes of thought and leaps straight from the problem to the answer. —Robert Graves

Trust your hunches. They are usually based on facts filed away just below the conscious level. —Joyce Brothers

En route to Honolulu with a stopover in Maui, I got swept away by the flow of life. One serendipitous event after another occurred. To begin with, I arrived at the gate about an hour early, and was offered a seat on the earlier flight. Big deal, it has probably happened to most of us. I was ahead of the schedule, and I said, "Yes." They promised my bag would come on the later flight. Something inside said, *'just go, keep moving in the direction of the wind.'* I did and expected to wait at the Honolulu Airport another hour for my bag. I arrived and decided to make use of my time and get a rental car while waiting for my luggage. I walked out to the median to pick up the shuttle bus and then my inner voice said, *'go back inside and check for the bag.'* I went back to baggage claim and there it was. I had listened and trusted the unseen—or guidance, intuition, insight, god's 'word.'

Small thing? Yes, it sure felt like intuition and the 'flow.' A close friend, the Ravendove, says "**Flow** (creativity) happens after practice, practice, and more practice." I interpret that to be exercising the trust muscle. That day in Honolulu, I knew there was no risk, my plan was set and therefore I had total trust that everything would work out. Because of this confidence I responded to the intuitive and it worked out.

Another example: One night while walking downtown Honolulu after dinner on the way to a local jazz joint, I decided to take an alternative street and discovered a jazz band at a totally different club. It was great, and we never bothered to go to the first place. We caught the scent of jazz in the tropical air, and responded with relaxed confidence.

No doubt these kinds of incidents happen all the time, and we don't pay attention. What if we strengthen our trust of the unseen, un-known, and unconscious, from these minor cases of intuition into bigger and bolder moves in business or relationships?

One time in preparation for an extended foreign trip, I did my due diligence and researched tours and flight options to that area. I was priming the pump to that possibility. I wanted to be attuned to that place. After the investigation, I noted three omens about that destination: 1) an email from a friend in Europe out of nowhere said he has a contact in that rarely trav-eled country, 2) a book based on the spirituality of its indigenous people was mentioned in a sermon by a minister, and 3) my all time favorite song in their language randomly played on my MP3 player—all within a few days. Coincidence? Power of attraction? Could be. When I notice those signs, I feel connected to my deeper, unconscious desires. (Update: I eventually took that trip to southern Africa, and it was a total success.)

By the fifth decade of life we have spent many years developing and relying on planning and analyzing. It may have rewarded us with financial security, success in our careers, and negotiating the material world. Most couldn't function well without this kind of thinking. But along with the benefit of rational thinking, there is a risk of boredom and cynicism. 'Been there, done that' thinking comes from doing things the way we always have. Who doesn't get stuck in habitual patterns and desire novel experiences?

Expansion and fulfillment increases when we open to the other messages that don't compute in the left brain. Strengthening the intuitive muscle has helped me to be more spontaneous, trusting, and decisive. Initially, a bit of anxiety may arise, but after years of following the signs, oracles, and omens, it has become comfortable. Make an experiment and see what happens when you give up of control and go with the flow of life.

Inner Journey:

☐ Recall moments of intuition: a phone call anticipated, a premonition about an event, or a coincidental meeting with a friend.

Action Steps:

☐ Spend a day looking for 'coincidences' and record them. Do you place any meaning to them?

☐ Ask an oracle a question that has been vexing you, then act on this guidance. See what happens, when you really do it.

Chapter 24
The Sweet Reward of Structured Spontaneity

It is a mistake to try to look too far ahead. The chain of destiny can only be grasped one link at a time.
— *Winston Churchill*

Take the first step in faith. You don't have to see the whole staircase—just take the first step.
— *Martin Luther King, Jr*

Trusting the omens, signs, intuitions, and guidance, I hit the road seeking new horizons and surprises. I planned to experiment with my new practice of recognizing and acting on intuition. The first challenge was to choose a specific goal and then to take action from the inner guidance, not mental analysis. In our modern culture of seemingly endless choice, the risk of *analysis paralysis* is always present (see *Paradox of Choice* by Barry Schwartz). I find it more so since leaving my full time career. It may be because I have more time to make the theoretically 'right' decision. I decided to strengthen the intuitive muscle with a field trip to San Diego. I had a two pronged strategy: 1) see friends and 2) practice tuning in to the flow.

Breaking out of the inertia of home and its comforts is never easy for me. Like many people, I will procrastinate on intended trips in ever complicating ways for days, months, maybe years. Getting started was the biggest hurdle. I've found it helpful to make plans, in ink. In this case, I made plans to visit friends who live in that area on a certain date. That got me on the road and in action. Throwing some gear in the car, I had an appointment and destination. The venue of my intuition practice was Ocean Beach, a bohemian/surf neighborhood near downtown San Diego.

I selected Ocean Beach because an herbal dispensary, Happy Herbs, I patronize has an outlet there. Rather than going directly to the address when I arrived, I chose to look around and get the vibe. After parking my car, I walked about one block and happened upon an esoteric practice that I had never seen in L.A. or anywhere . . . *chakra balancing.*

Synchronistically, I had recently done a week-long workshop based on the chakra model. I enthusiastically said "yes," and within a few minutes I was in the 'treatment' room, planetarium style décor with stars in the sky. Almost immediately, the 'balancer' said she saw red, indicating inflammation, around my lower back (I have been diagnosed with acute herniated and bulging discs throughout my lumbar and sacrum). Right on.

Buoyed by this experience, I continued my exploration of Ocean Beach with an expectant and receptive mind. From there it was an easy walk to coffee lounges, used CD stores, and hip restaurants. Strolling around the neighborhood felt so familiar. My kind of place. I walked to the main shopping street before going to the herbal shop which was supposed to be on a different street. Sud-denly, about one block down the street after the surf shop, the coffee lounge, and the used cd store, I spied the herb store.

They had moved to this street. After purchasing some herbs and making plans to reconnect with the proprietor back home in Venice, I discovered the weekly farmer's market. There it was again, *the right place at the right time*. A fine street band playing my favorite music and friendly street scene capped the evening.

Breaking out of the routines of life gets more challenging the older we are. For the newly retired, it can be like the proverbial convict who returns to jail because it is his comfort zone. Liberation from the job doesn't always liberate the spirit. Since we are all pattern seekers, structures and routines in life comfort and ground us. But unchecked, they can lead to a large dose of ennui. The breaking of set and the resulting novelty stimulates the mind and emotions. Escaping from habituated mentality fuels reinvention and renewed passion for life.

Scientific studies show that the happiness that stays with us is experiential, not new possessions. The most impactful (even when unpleasant at the time) experiences are often are those connections with places and/or people that were unplanned. Don't wait for the big trip, the big romance, the big job, but go for whatever attracts your discerning eye. Then, set up a structure that provides the necessary degree of comfort and push the edges to the unknown and unpredictable. Trust your intuition to point the way and blast off. Arriving at the goal, it may be that the real boon is unexpected people, places, and events that just happened.

Inner Journey:

☐ Remember a trip you took that was totally planned, complete with hotels, buses, meals, break time. What do you recall that was not on the itinerary?

Action Steps:

☐ Plan a day out of town with an outline of the plan, hotel, sights or persons to visit with plenty of time to explore. Then let your instinct or intuition lead you.

Chapter 25
Karma Pays Off in Music to my Ears

*By letting go it all gets done. The world is won by those
who let it go. But when you try and try, the world is beyond
winning.*   *—Lao Tzu*

What goes around, comes around.
       —Anonymous

Bang, rattle, bang, I look up from my computer. At the door was
an older gentleman (90+) I've become friendly with over the past
year saying good morning when he passes my house walking his
dog. I looked up from my solo study of my favorite topics: self-
improvement and getting organized. The first I have pursued for
over thirty years with varying success (maybe more if I include
my recently found essays as a middle-school student). The
second maybe genetic—my 86-year-old father still bemoans the
fact that he is not organized.

My relationship with both of these efforts has been rife with
struggles, sinkholes, and successes. My personal/spiritual growth
path has ranged from the est training to Siddha Yoga to zen to
talk therapy to men's mytho-poetics to flotation tanks. A long
and winding road and not always the road less traveled. In a

symbiotic relationship, my genetic disposition to be organization-ally challenged and the self-improvement path are twin poles around a core self that yearns for understanding and community.

Clutter or disorganization is largely in the eyes of the beholder. Metaphysical teachers claim that the excess stuff blocks the energy flow to bring the new. When I feel stuck occasionally I leave my jam-packed home and visit an empty, sterile motel room for empty space. I have noted a family tradition, from my grandparents to my father, to my own constantly growing stuff. If we annually collect the same amount of stuff, from, say, age 20 to 60, we end up with a shitload of papers, souvenirs, and a wide variety of tshotsches.

Lately, I have been on a mission to cleanse, purge, release, or trash, items formerly stored in boxes in the attic. Because of this mis-sion, areas of my house that would normally be free and clear of clutter are filled with piles of boxes, papers, and electronic bric a brac. Yesterday, I examined some stuff that had lain around my office for months. I perused, sorted, and trashed a bunch of old student papers, letters (remember those time capsules?), cancelled concert tickets, posters, and photos.

Yeh! Feeling elated and looking at a bright, clear day here at the beach and I decided to reward myself with a bike ride listening to my mp3 player with its six thousand+ songs.

I couldn't find it and frustration had me running around the house; high and low, inside and outside the house, the car, and the yard. No Zune player to be found, then acceptance kicked in. Changing my mind I elected to relax and hope to find the player tomorrow. I let it go and had a fine ride at the beach. It sparked memories of Hawaii and my long cherished dream of moving there. I have had a fascination with Hawaii since sixth grade (in the cleanup I purged old school reports about Hawaii), and have visited Maui several times since retiring.

Back to the rude interruption from my elderly neighbor who is very hard of hearing, I jumped up and with probably a trace of annoyance in my voice said, "Hi. What is up?" He replied, "I have been trying to find you for days, and you haven't been here. I found a music player on the sidewalk and figured it must be yours." I thank him profusely and immediately walked with him to his house. While waiting outside, I saw a sign in Hawaiian I inquired about that and he told me that they used to go to Maui every year for fifteen years until his wife took ill a few years ago—to me, more evidence of the web that connects all of us and a demonstration of personal karma in the present.

My bottom line goal is peace of mind. I practice meditation to enhance that state. Science documents practical benefits in physical health, emotional health, creativity, sleep, weigh control, and many other areas. In the midst of the stress I felt equanamous and got to take the bike ride with six thousand songs.

Inner Journey:

☐ When did you receive unexpected good?
Did you somehow set up the conditions for
that boon?

Action Steps:

☐ Gift someone anonymously.

☐ Say hello to everyone you pass on the street
for one day.

Chapter 26
Finding and Riding the Flow and Avoiding the Eddies

The characteristic feature of . . . synchronistic occurrences is meaningful coincidence, and as such I have defined the synchronistic principle. This principle suggests that there is an inter-connection or unity of causally unrelated events, and thus postulates a unitary aspect of being which can very well be described as the 'unus mundus' [one world].
— C. G. Jung

Don't let your brain interfere with your heart.
— Albert Einstein

Relaxing into my first soak in the storied hot baths at *Esalen*, I heard a shout from a young woman surrounded by several naked soakers. "What does your tattoo mean?" I explained, and she said, "Oh yes. I am a follower of that." A few minutes pass, while I gazed out to the undulating Pacific Ocean and its dense forest of underwater kelp. Then a different young woman said that she, too, is a student of that spiritual philosophy. A lively and animated conversation developed and before I knew it, she suggested I visit her at the restaurant where she works. I respond "of course", which really means maybe in my mind.

Energized and clear after a week at Esalen, we drove to Berkeley and planned to spend one night. The next day I decided to eat at the Café Gratitude, where the young woman in the tub worked. My companion, an old college friend, The Runner, on this trip challenged me, "Why do you want to go there? Are you hitting on that girl?" In my mind I had no further thought than to continue a positive connection begun in the baths. Café Gratitude is a chain of seven restaurants which support positive and healthy living through affirmations on the walls and menus and fully, organic vegetarian food. The food is excellent and the vibe even better. Well worth following the 'sign' from the tubs.

Later that day, after meeting some Berkeley friends for drinks, we debated where to go--San Francisco or Berkeley? Standing at the BART station we were about to drop into a familiar pattern of manly men: 'Whose will wins?' Then the young lady from Esalen and the café appeared out of the dusk on her way to San Fran-cisco to do a street art performance. Seizing this clear direction, we go with her and had an exciting and fun time in the Mission District with its nouveau hip ambience. Later, we hit North Beach and its mix of strip clubs and post-beatniks. City Lights Bookstore served up a healthy dose of authentic paper books of poets and other counter-culturalists. While at the "Hungry I" on the other hand, a string of luscious young ladies in skimpy attire and big smiles paraded.

Noting and responding to such 'coincidences' is a practice of mine. A theory explaining correspondence is called synchronicity, which was developed by one of the towering figures of psychol-ogy in the 20th century, Carl Gustav Jung (Swiss 1875–1961). Jung's investigations into the occult and Eastern thought led him to postulate the theory of acausal connectivity. In his framework, connections between places, things, and people may be non-linear or *acausal*. Their relationships may be understood as parts of a field as opposed to a linear cause and effect. When we experience in those moments of 'meaningful coincidence,' we experience a connection in the web of existence.

We have all had them---the phone call from someone just after we thought of that person or the sense of déjà' vu of some place we have never been. Accessing and using this field is alien to most trained in the Western mind-set of scientific Newtonian/ Cartesian thought. My boundaries of analytic thinking softened a bit by the communality of Esalen. Trusting and tapping into this field rewarded me with serendipitous experiences.

The next day for the first time in forty years of traveling, the hotel was booked for that night, and we had to leave. Nearby hotels were also booked or exorbitant. With ease and minimal analysis, I said, "It is time to leave" to my rolling partner and he protested, "How come? You are too easily swayed." I know me and my stubbornness to follow my will, but this time I choose to trust my guidance. We left, and it felt right on time.

Seeing the flow of life and surrendering to its clear messages always pushes me. I am not naturally intuitive and my tendency is to analyze an issue, then do a lengthy cost-benefit analysis, and flip a coin. Then begin the process all over, with doubt and remorse. Needless to say, this approach can be time-consuming, may not lead to the best outcomes, and encourages second thoughts. Fed up with analysis paralysis, I resolved to note the signs, feelings, omens, and then, as Nike used to say, "Just Do It." Each day offers clues to the natural flow and that makes my life so much easier.

Inner Journey:

☐ Take some time to reflect on synchronistic event from your life. What did it mean to you?

Action Steps:

☐ Pay attention in your life for a week and see if you can identify some synchronicities.

☐ Meditate on some person or thing for a few days and see what happens.

'Feel like I'm Fixin' to Die'
—Country Joe McDonald

PART 5.
DEMONS: FUNK, PERFECTIONISM & DOUBT

Chapter 27
Unpack Your Baggage and Restart Your Engine

A person who has never made a mistake has never tried anything new. —Albert Einstein

By confronting our failures, we come closer to reaching perfection. —Scott Beare

Crowds in the central square of Cairo, placards exhorting the dictator to be gone, and TV news reporters scurrying for cover— deja' vu all over again. Another *peoples'* revolution expressing frustration with a rapacious autocrat. Pushed to the edge of starvation and desperate for a voice, they banded together to express their frustration and somehow found the courage to hope for positive change. Politicians burnished their image by supporting civil rights and behind the scenes negotiated with the dictator. They succeeded, the old regime fell and a new strong-man took over. But the odds against major systemic change are long. Real revolutions are rarer than a winner in Vegas.

From the Arab Spring to affluent beach living in California, great instability pervades this era. The old axiom that all politics is local applies to the personal as well. Real change always begins with the individual. The transition into the third life stage (post-work) shook my inner foundation. Just as Mubarak learned that change was inevitable, I realized big changes in my lifestyle were certain and desirable. Breaking out of an entrenched system of friends, habits, and routines prompted an eruption in my soul and a busting out of the comfort zone that limited growth. Three years on into my 'reinvention,' I found myself in a dark place.

Waking with a sense of futility and doubt, I thought--- What is the point of reinvention? Where does it lead anyway? Do I still have the will to follow through to the other side of anxiety and fear? Is this an unavoidable element of aging? Perhaps, but how do I manage this mood in order to continue my mission of reinvention?

Reinventors often face this question: How do I negotiate and persist through the likely moments of aridity and self doubt? The challenge of age added another layer that is not present when we are young and fresh. Over the years experiences and lessons or 'baggage' accumulate. Unpacking that heavy load yielded insights and strategies to continue the journey. I grouped the 'baggage' into four types; 'been there, done that,' 'Too old/tired/ stupid to' (start over, learn something new, move), 'My life is comfortable, so why bother,' and finally 'what if I fail?'

Where did these ideas and feelings come from? My *interpreta-tions* of most likely *faulty* memories. It is almost automatic to analyze events in our lives. Often those incidents carry some sort of emotional charge. One day I awoke with my old friend 'been there, done that.' I chose to dive into that enervating feeling and poke around. In the muck, I uncovered an attitude cobbled together from bits and pieces of frustration from my former job, hobbies, and relationships. Even though I hold a generally favor-able view of those experiences, discomfort was also there and this disquiet popped up and infected my intention to reinvent, renew, and refire my life.

My tonic was to write about those disappointments to make sense of them. By shaping a narrative of my life, I no longer felt helpless. I regained my power. After unpacking the old unresolved pain, leaping into the unknown was not so frightening. In fact, it was exhilarating.

'I am too old' or 'It's too late' is probably the most pernicious of these viruses. In our culture, aging is not generally seen by as a good thing. But the life cycle must end and aging is part of it. That fact can't be disputed but it shouldn't stop our growth and fun in the process. As we age, learning new skills slows but, the benefit maybe a heightened appreciation of the moment or mindfulness. But a useful goal needs clarity of mission and vision. When those three elements are clear, then taking the necessary steps is easier. Each is worthy of in-depth discussion, but one definition of mission is how one puts his/her unique gifts, skills, and talents in service to others. Vision describes the form that mission takes in the material realm. Finally, goals are the specific projects to be accomplished. When the excuses of doubt and lack are seen in this light, then the value of mission overrides the personal limitations.

By the time we reach AARP age, we've all made many, many mistakes and suffered myriad failures. But when they are held in the embrace of compassion, then wisdom can arise. Failure is a part of life. But failures can propel us to learn and prosper. It takes wisdom to make practical solutions out of moments of failure. Failure is not a static event. It is a point of view. Checking our circumstances with wisdom, we can then take steps that are practical and progressive.

On this day I joined Lazarus and got up from the dead of ennui and walked. I walked to the café and met a fellow late-in-life reinventor and creative. His example started my engine. I remembered my **Mission, Vision, and Goals** and I'm moving again.

Inner Journey:

☐ Recall a major event in your life that you consider a failure. With the cold, clear eye of time, did you quit too easily? Why?

☐ Reframe an incident from your life that you still give yourself a hard time. Think about how it contributed to your life.

Action Steps:

☐ Write: 1) the mission, the qualities that having it would give you, 2) vision: what it looks like in detail, including the look, smells, and sensations, and 3) specific interim goals.

Chapter 28

Once a Hippie or
Don't Bogart that Joint

*Have patience with all things, but chiefly have patience
with yourself. Do not lose courage in considering your own
imperfections but instantly set about remedying them—
every day begin the task anew.*

—*St. Francis de Sales*

*Man's main task in life is to give birth to himself, to become
what he potentially is.* —*Erich Fromm*

One bright sunny day I craved a dose of country and nostalgia
and found it less than a half hour from my home in Venice. Winding through the Santa Monica Mountains, I passed a crystal store
and had a flashback of an old friend from college days. Whatever
happened to Steve S.? He loved Topanga and all aspects of the
hippie culture.

Always an early adopter, he introduced us to marijuana and then
various other consciousness-altering substances. As teenage
suburbanites, we yearned to get out of the housing tracts and
into the bucolic bohemian vibe of Topanga. Many weekends we
would race through there in my little red Triumph sports car and
stumble upon parties, love-ins, and bacchanals. In those communal days, as long as you were wearing the appropriate
threads (clothes), you were welcome. No invitation needed. It
was the era of free love, community, and free expression.

An old friend reported that Steve S. had pursued a career with the unemployment department in state government. Searching Facebook, I found him, and we 'friended.' It turned out he, too, had recently retired and was now free from the daily work grind. Always musically oriented (he was a major fan of Rod Stewart), he used to play guitar in college. I figured he would be playing a lot of guitar and taking a lot of foreign trips (he once did the mythical and mystical overland trip from London to Kabul, Afghanistan).

We arranged to meet at the classic Topanga restaurant, *Inn of the Seventh Ray*, to talk old times. With tables overlooking Topanga Creek, the *Inn* is a Topanga institution with healthy organic food and even better atmosphere, serene and in nature.

My overt and sincere agenda was to catch up with an old friend; my covert motive was to see how he was faring in 'retirement' given my own rocky transition. We had had similar experiences with secure, highly structured careers in government service that led to pensions, we grew up in the suburbs, and we were comrades in the cultural revolution of the '70s. Our paths diverged when he transferred to San Diego State and I went to UC Berkeley. He eventually joined the Employment Development Dept (after years wandering around the world), and I became a teacher and administrator with LAUSD. We had a lot in common —Nothing like friends from one's formative years.

After catching up on the past thirty years, we discussed the challenge of productively managing time. With the lack of imposed structure, his new lifestyle presented unexpected dilemmas and rewards similar to mine. But the issue that hit him by surprise was our old mutual friend—cannabis. He related his dance with the herb, like it was a long-lost-girl friend. Still loves her but has a hard time sorting out the mixed emotions of attraction, fun, and addiction.

Posted over the creek, listening to the bull frogs, and watching the hummingbirds, we got down to the real deal. Turned out he goes on binges of ingesting marijuana every day for weeks at a time and then goes on the wagon. In order to stop, he'll go out of town for a couple weeks. Then upon return, the siren calls, and its easy entertainment and comfort is too much to resist. Betty Bong beckons, and he fires up again. She seduces him like Salome and her seven veils. At times she excites and thrills and other times the habit saps energy and will. What troubles Steve is that he has worked for thirty years to have the freedom to do what he wants, and he likes to get high. But that ostensibly benign pleasure has become problematic for him.

It has been reported that with the aging and retiring of the Boomer generation, the old bongs have been dusted off and more weed is consumed by the now old ex-hippies. So, it isn't a situation unique to my old friend. Many questions arise out of this dynamic:

1. Managing and limiting use when the usual constraints (job, kids in the house) are gone.
2. Health considerations when old habits are imposed on an older body (hangovers, excessive eating—'munchies').
3. Possibly enhanced fun and patience in learning new skills,
4. Integrating the emotional and spiritual insights into the latter stage of life.

The struggle of my successful, affluent, professional friend is not rare. The journey of older life is often filled with indulging in preferred recreations. It may also be a time of spiritual questing and discovery. New or long-dormant interests in creativity can at last be explored. Coming from a pleasure-seeking generation in the '70s, it seemed natural. But at this age I needed to thread the needle between an experience that reveals and expresses deep-seated desires and a sacrilegious excess that leads to escapism and dependence. The option is the redemption and reward for all we aspired to in our youth or a descent into delusion and escape. By the way, the reefer habit could be replaced with any pleasure done to excess, food, travel, alcohol, yoga, shopping. The challenge is to find the mix that satisfies, but doesn't inhibit making the most of this new freedom that we've earned.

Inner Journey:

☐ What are your dreams for 'retirement?'
What are vices that potentially could waylay
your dreams?

☐ Meditate on what you want to further accomplish in your life? Learn a language? Visit
certain countries? Build a new business or a
creative art?

Action Steps:

☐ If you are retired from 'work', note how
your time is spend for one week. Analyze it
and assess what needs to be changed to
work toward your life goals.

Chapter 29
After the Valley of Darkness, the Sun Shines

Challenges make you discover things about yourself that you never really knew. They're what make the instrument stretch—what makes you go beyond the norm.
                    —Cicely Tyson

Never give up while there is hope; but hope not beyond reason for that shows more desire than judgment.
                    —William Penn

Believe it or not the sun doesn't always shine in Southern California. Especially at the beach where I live the marine layer, rolls in on an almost daily basis. The sun's beacon again was shrouded, as I sat on my new front porch/lanai/deck/stoop. Inside my soul was as dark as my favorite dessert—brownies. The funk had started a few months earlier, when I reserved a trip to a writer's conference in Cape Cod. Immediately, a worm insinuated itself into my subconscious—nerves, anxiety, worry, and trepidation. There wasn't any presenting issue; it simply arose in my aware-ness one day.

For months, each day had been in slow motion, as if I dragged around a fifty-pound psychic weight. The mood lifted a bit doing simple chores, trim the tree in the yard, clean the bathroom, take the computer for servicing. But in the quiet and solitary times, the yawning maw of the dark beckoned. It bellowed its siren song of warning. *Don't go there, don't do that, watch out for him,* (and most vexing), *why bother?*

I retraced my twisting life trail of the last couple years and realized most of the time I was lost in Rumi's poem, *The Tavern*, 'if I could taste one sip of an answer, I could break out of this prison for drunks.' I was helpless, clueless, and deep in the pit and waiting for Godot to save me.

I am not alone. Most of us do many things to avoid falling in that sinkhole. Fifty million American adults are on anti-depressant medications, 25 million regular cannabis users (4+ times per month) and 30 million regular drinkers (4+ times per week). Of course, there is much overlap in these altered state individuals but that doesn't even include the other forms of self-medicating, obesity, compulsive shopping, gambling, or sometimes (my Marxist college professors would be pleased) religion. Whatever gets you through the night? Regardless, clearly a lot of us seek escape from emotional pain. But often the depression or stress or dissatisfaction often boils down to 'what's life about?' Can there be one person over 40 who hasn't had this thought?

Finding an answer has been my mission for years—decades! Now, a few years into my so-called 'retirement,' I've had the house remodeled, made many trips out of town, stayed out late every night of the week, volunteered, and took art and guitar classes. I bounced from one dabble to another. No 'purpose' or 'meaning' did I find. Like a character in a Fassbinder movie, first my spirits soared, then my head spun like an inner gyroscope gone amuck, then inertia set in. The abyss, my journey to the center of the soul, beckoned.

Even in my darkest times, routine kept me going--- gym, meditation, family, and house maintenance. But I had no 'joie de vivre,' no enthusiasm, no hope of the future—all AWOL. My long nurtured visions of living on a tropical island, finding a life companion, and contributing to social change had faded, no longer dreams I was working on but mere fantasies. No more real than a night dream.

Friends see me as a Buddha of patience, but a lifelong challenge has been to really appreciate the present experience. I always figured that 'new and different' would mean more fun and freer. I just kept moving on. The unknown offered possibility and hope. Who knows what will happen? Fueled by this innate curiosity and bias for novelty, I was never bored. Then I arrived in this darkest of valleys: the grass was no longer greener over there—futility. And it hit me: *From the widest angle, life is never **better,** just different*. Stuff began to shift that day.

That morning the sun broke through the haze and zapped my soul. I caught the wave. Surrendering to the momentum, at last connected to the life source, I was alive again. Well, not that I was dead before, but the time of agitation and fear churned my inner waters. But when the wave hit, a rush of energy coursed through my soul, even though I knew that it too would pass.

Is there a shortcut through the valley of doubt, fear, and insecurity? If there is, I haven't found it in 30+ years of study and effort. I think it comes with being human, especially for those middle-aged and older individuals who strike out into new and challenging work and art. Skills built over a lifetime are put aside and the subconscious 95% of our mind is free to bubble up to the surface. And where there was once competence and confidence (our jobs, family), doubt and vulnerability emerge. At that point we get to grow or retreat to the comfortable. For a while I longingly gazed back at my former routine and job, but realized that life is gone like my old, out-of-fashion suits. For me there is only one path—*growth-learning-adventure-expansion.* Inevitably, sometimes that road leads through a valley of darkness.

I still have days of doubt and fear but when it happens I know in my soul that tomorrow WILL be DIFFERENT and probably better. I remember my mantra: *Pay attention, keep stepping, breathe deeply, and give thanks.* Somehow even when things don't change a lot, they seem better.

Inner Journey:

☐ Remember a time of depression? What finally got you out of it?

☐ Stop, look, and listen to what is going on right now in front of you and inside of you and embrace it all.

Action Steps:

☐ Take action on a long-delayed goal.

☐ Be of service to someone in particular.

Chapter 30
Reggae Colors Mean: Stop, Look, Go

One love, one heart one destiny . . . let's get together and feel alright. —Bob Marley

All I needed to know, I learned in kindergarten. —Robert Fulgum

The crowd of 15,000 was on its 30,000 feet and singing along with the performers to a song that was a hit forty years ago. Looking around you could see '70ish couples and newlywed twenty-somethings with their infants. In my row, a group of apparent Polynesian ancestry had two full ice chests of beer and across the walkway was a stylishly dressed woman in her 60's who was dancing with a man in a wheelchair.

After nearly three hours, the crowd roared as one for the encore by the band who began in the 1960s and included son of reggae icon, Bob Marley, and his mother Rita Marley. It was a transcendent moment that expressed Marley's vision of 'one love, one heart, one people, one destiny.' In the nearly one hundred-year-old Hollywood Bowl, the walls of our social categories vanished and humanity exposed its core. Separations by ethnicity, age, and class were all left at the turnstiles and we were together. Drawn together by music that proclaims freedom from 'isms' and schisms, harmony and free spirits prevailed. When Bob Marley performed you did not see this wildly heterogeneous crowd. Back in the '70's his audience was nearly all young, long-haired white kids.

This joyous celebration highlighted an important aspect to my reinvention: ***Adjust to changed circumstances***. I used to be a regular summertime fan of the Hollywood Bowl, but in recent years traffic congestion and parking frustration had risen to a breaking point, and I quit going. I crossed the Bowl off my list of venues and passed on many good shows. Enticed out of my lassitude and negative attitude by my close friend, Ras Herm, to see a once-in-a-lifetime pairing of Ziggy Marley and the I-Threes, I took a chance. Instead of fighting the transportation issues, we took the shuttle bus with a few other friends. No stress coming or going. Get on the bus with your ice chest and dinner, chit chat en route, and relax into the irie (joyous) spirit.

The show was an absolute treat from start to finish. MC'd by Ziggy, it began promptly on time, ended on time and included massive video screens and powerful acoustics. Peers of Bob Marley, Ras Michael, the Wailing Souls, and the Mighty Diamonds played their classic and anthemic songs. By the time the I-Threes appeared we were primed. Each note was perfect as their solos and harmonies soared on classic Bob Marley songs and their personal hits. By the time Ziggy came on, the crowd was on its feet, moving as one body to the beat and living up to his lyric "Look Whose Dancing Now."

As great as the music was, even greater was the camaraderie of 15,000 brothers and sisters. Musing on this splendid evening, I realized how my old method of doing the Bowl limited my potential for pleasure. Breaking out of that cage and adjusting to the changed conditions allowed me to have a fun evening with my tribe. A potential downside of age and experience is that sometimes I think I have it figured out and follow an old script. Additionally, because things have changed, they no longer serve me. It could be in friendships, jobs, homes, sports, you name it. Now, I brake, look for a different approach, and open the door once again. The reggae colors of red, gold, and green mean to me: Stop, Look, Go and into life.

Inner Journey:

☐ Review your life for activities or friends you discontinued because conditions changed. Were the changes irreparable? Could a new approach be taken?

☐ When was the last time you felt connected with a crowd of people?

Action Steps:

☐ Take one of those activities or friends that ended and brainstorm how to redo it.

☐ Next time you start to reject an activtity you used to enjoy, practice---stop, reflect, and act.

Chapter 31
Wiping Out and Getting Back on the Board

We are made to persist. That's how we find out who we are.
                                        —*Tobias Wolff*

What is defeat? Nothing but education; nothing but the first step to something better.
                                        —*Wendell Phillips*

Bending over to pick up a bag I felt a shooting pain from my upper arm into the shoulder. Instantly, I knew it was back, the shoulder injured almost a month ago in Hawaii. Two days later the doctor's diagnosis: Muscle strain. Treatment? Rest and ibuprofen. How many times have I heard that since I turned 50? Having been athletic all my life, now the aches and pains from decades of wear and tear show up regularly and unexpectedly. This one started after stand-up paddle surfing in Waikiki. Strangely, it was not a specific incident but the strain of an hour in the water. Two nights later, I awoke in the middle of the night with a throbbing pain in my right shoulder. Only a regular regimen of pain killers got me through the next ten days. When the doctor prescribed rest and ibuprofen, he admonished "Just don't do anything that hurts." Brilliant, I thought sarcastically!

Eventually, feeling pretty good and I went to the gym to do minor stretches and lifting. Picking up the light gym bag, the strain came back. Damn! In spite of certain advantages to aging, changes in the body usually means adjusting, slowing down, or elimination of activities.

Sometimes while you're learning a new sport, as I was on the stand up board in Hawaii, you can wipe out on a *Big Rock*, Stephen Covey's term for the barriers on one's road to happiness. You can't go around the rock or blow it up. You can simply quit and say you're too old, or lie and say you didn't want to do it anyway. But the bold Boomer forges ahead, armed with the wisdom of experience and knows the most effective and rewarding approach is to chip away at it until it is not in the way. It may still be there, but step around it, or over it, or on it. I find when doctors prescribe a treatment plan, the recovery takes about four times longer than it did twenty years ago. I could pretend I'm still 25 or 35 and jump back in and likely reinjure. Or take a cue from meditation and practice mindfulness. Just simmer down. Don't turn off the fire but turn it down.

Patience is mandatory for physical healing and learning a sport or skill. Just as the body heals slower in later life, the muscle memory needed for skill development is slower. The body, brain, and muscles need more time to learn new skills. Taking up a new sport or even returning to an old sport requires a different approach physically and emotionally. I wondered how to approach a new passion such as stand-up paddle surfing?

Self-Determination Theory offers a good template for building momentum for a new interest. A widely practiced theory of motivation, it posits three elements for happiness in any domain of life:

1. Autonomy
2. Competence
3. Relatedness.

Recognizing how these three elements factor into building satisfaction or fulfillment provides a clue for what can be done to keep up the interest. An injured surfer might need to up the ante on **Relatedness,** since the activity is usually solitary and high on the **Autonomy** scale. The **Competency** aspect is reduced, since the injury requires stopping skill development for awhile. Perhaps there could be book to study until one is physically able. Relatedness is similar to community. Relatedness in this case may be joining a local club or reading a hobbyist magazine or going to an online chat room.

Usually people just wait out the injury and do nothing for awhile, but there is risk in that approach. Once bitten, twice shy. Waiting a few months to renew the activity or sport and you may find the ardor has dimmed. Since people are hard-wired to be novelty, seekers it is tempting to just move on.

Sliding through the autumn of my life into the winter, I encounter changes in all areas of life, from work to sports to avocations to relationships to sex. It is life—all things must pass. Physical and mental decline are part of the journey of life. I cope with my back issue by doing everything I can to mitigate the decline—exercise, diet, meditation, and so on. I strive to be real and at the same time by working on **competence** (learning), **relatedness** (community), and **autonomy** (personal choice). I jump on the board and when I fall, get back up and ride the wave wherever it goes.

Inner Journey:

☐ Recall a new activity or sport that you attempt-
ed, failed and quit. Why did you stop? Make a
list of the activities you quit before becoming
competent.

☐ Now remember something that was difficult at
first but which you pushed through to competence (learning a language, typing, driving).

Action Steps:

☐ Sign up for classes in something you have
always wanted to learn (guitar, tango, Portuguese). Do it for at least 10 weeks or sessions.
Track your feelings weekly, i.e. frustrated, fun,
exhilarated. Celebrate at the end and reflect on
the competence you have gained.

Chapter 32
Banish Perfectionism, Welcome 'Good Enough'

Striving for perfection is the greatest stopper there is . . .
It's your excuse to yourself for not doing anything. Instead,
strive for excellence, doing your best.
—Sir Laurence Olivier

Twenty years from now, you will be more disappointed by
the things you didn't do than by the ones you did do.
—Mark Twain

Over thirty years ago, one, warm, summer day around sunset
I walked up to a big tent on a parking lot on Ocean Ave., Santa
Monica. Now three 5-star luxury hotels fill that spot. At the vesti-
bule stood a dozen devotees wearing saris and other Indian garb,
who welcomed me with the traditional palms together Indian
greeting—*namaste*. Next to the door was a huge glass barrel
about 10 feet high which was filled with hash pipes, cigarettes,
syringes, and liquor bottles. I asked, "What is that about?" A dev-
otee responded, "Baba absorbs karma because he is a perfected
being." Firmly in my 'prove it' attitude, I sat through the program
of chanting and a discourse by Muktananda in Hindi translated,
into English by the attractive, young assistant who succeeded him.

Eventually, I had the opportunity for darshan (blessing) with the
guru and walked up to the podium and looked in his eyes. What

I saw was beyond the mind or the material world. This little, old Indian man with the orange beanie was the first and only person I have ever met who alleged enlightenment. That began my quest to know and to achieve awakening or perfection.

Perfectionism: a personal belief that anything less than perfect is undesirable.

After Swami Muktananda died, stories came out about his less than perfect behavior with devotees. Like the rest of us, it turns out he had foibles. Throughout my life I have oppressed myself with perfectionism in the important domains of life: mate, job, home, health. Never fully satisfied, I too often changed the job or the girl because it or she wasn't perfect. Never satisfied, the grass was always greener. I once had a therapist who admonished me to not drop a girlfriend as long as positives were more than the negatives (providing there were no deal breakers). I dropped him, not the girl.

American culture is suffused with perfectionist ideology. *Winner take all, second place is for losers, die trying.* What if there is no perfect, no absolute, and that date or job or house or suit of clothes was simply "good enough." Would it change your life? Would you be happier? Goals motivate us to improve and are an important component of happiness. But more, better, best can lead to constant striving, never arriving.

Let's back up a bit. As Boomers, we have been exhorted to live our dreams all of our lives. The Boomer generation was indulged by parents who had suffered deprivation in the Great Depression and World War II. As youths, we felt entitled to be, do, and have what we wanted. We wanted perfection. That zeitgeist fit with the traditional American spirit of self-reliance. Later, many joined the human potential movement.

Since Emerson, a fringe element of American culture, the self-improvement industry expanded into the mainstream in the '70s with the neo-zen *est* training, which promised instant transformation. Naturally, after you've been transformed you want the perfect mate, job, house, and body. Self-help reached some sort of zenith with Oprah Winfrey and her massive TV following. Coincidentally, Oprah ended her show in the aftermath of the Great Recession. Perhaps that economic challenge heralded a new perspective on the search for perfection.

American self-help/personal growth did not start in the '60's or '70's but can be traced all the way back to Jefferson's 'pursuit of happiness' as enshrined in the Declaration of Independence. Throughout our history, salesmen of perfection have achieved huge success, from James Allen's '*As Man Thinketh*' to Dale Carnegie's '*How to Win Friends and Influence People*' to Napoleon Hill's '*Think and Grow Rich*.' In the '80's these classic American success teachings coalesced in religion with televangelists such as Rev. Ike and Rev. Terry Cole-Whitaker. They offered a spiritual basis for enjoying 'heaven on earth.' Rev. Terry's slogan declared 'Prosperity Is Your Divine Right' and Rev. Ike promoted, 'Green Power.'

They said god wanted everyone to have a perfect life. So, when one brand or mate turns out to be a bit difficult, maybe it's time to recycle. After all, wasn't I promised heaven on earth? When a boss tries to get me to come to work on time, shouldn't I be following my divine right livelihood as an actor? The twin traps of choice and perfectionism ensnares the ungrounded, the gullible, and the dreamers. You can be sure another slick entrepreneur of optimal living lies in wait down the street with a new program or miracle cure for all that ails you. With effort, anyone can have perfection, just take another seminar or potion.

Pursuing the carrot of excellence has a place but you have to know when the donkey has gone far enough. Finally tired of looking for the ultimate job, mate, home, or health, I quit constant striving for perfection and never being content. I decided it was time to stop, assess, and appreciate the here and now. As the renowned meditation teacher, Akasa Levi of Santa Monica says **'good enough enlightenment.'**

Pursuing heaven on earth may be as valid as any other life purpose. But at that last seminar/sermon and last back of the room book table, I don't want to say I've missed *real* life in all of its glory and imperfections. These days, when I am tired of reading, studying, and workshopping about life, like Kazantzakis' Zorba the Greek, I get up and sing, play, and dance. That is *good enough*!

Inner Journey:

☐ What is the topic that you constantly study and don't do? What keeps you in never arriving?

☐ Are you a perfectionist? How?

Action Steps:

☐ Take the time one day to notice the perfection in the imperfect. Look at the plants with their stunted branches or the Ferrari that is at the mechanic. Now, do something publicly and purposely fail.

'Come on people, let's get
together and love one another'
—Youngbloods (Powers)

PART 6.
COMMUNITY

Chapter 33
Busting Free and into Community

It is confidence in our bodies, minds, and spirits that allows us to keep looking for new adventures, new directions to grow in and new lessons to learn.
—Oprah Winfrey

Community cannot long feed on itself; it can only flourish with the coming of others from beyond: their unknown and undiscovered sisters and brothers.
—Howard Thurman

Racing down the ski hill, wind in my face, muscle memory kicked in. I suddenly realized that the ski run could symbolize my life. *Constant* corrections, *unconscious* corrections, *skillful* corrections that rapid fire like cylinders in a car. Up down, left right, forward back. And before I knew it, I was at the bottom of the hill. Hardly a conscious thought occurred, the ride was a thrill, and I made it to the bottom. Trust can be a slippery thing. I have a high degree of trust in my skiing ability. Now, in my sixties, I raced down this easy hill. I used to get bored with this kind of mountain—no challenge. But this time finding those nooks and crannies of trust embedded in my body and soul added up to a fulfilling day.

That day on the ski hill happened, because I felt stuck. Stuck like a cat chasing its tail. Going around and around in circles with less and less energy. Getting less and less done and feeling worse and worse about myself. Finally, tired of my excuses, I jumped in the car and headed north 75 miles to the San Gabriel mountains. Breaking free of my routine, the neighborhood, and obligations, I cracked the egg. Rolling at 70 mph, the confusion of too many options, too many unfinished projects, and too much 'been there done that' evaporated. My all-time favorite song came on, and upon hearing the chorus to *One Love* sung in Zulu, tears flowed. Bottled up emotions poured out, I was in that juicy space where soul lives. Soulful feeling and truth leaked out in the familiar words. Harmonious voices singing in a rainbow of languages highlighted one of my core values and needs: **Community.**

On the ski hill I joined the mid-week tribe of dedicated skiers and boarders. Ninety percent were boarders and around one- third of my age. But I was with a community of mountain lovers who enjoy the thrill of racing down a snowy mountain. Leaning into that long entrenched body memory of carving ski turns on the snow was satisfying even though not novel. I was glad to be in the familiar experience but this time with the more relaxed atti-tude of maturity. I appreciated what I could do now and not hold onto an old model that is out of date. I no longer pushed myself past the limits of my ability, but even so the knees started to give out in a few hours. I had to relax and find the groove of easy slid-ing down the mountain and trust the body to know what to do. Hitting that inner place was liberating. I realized that I don't have to try to do what I did years ago—I call it *creative aging*.

I rode the chair lift with a couple boarders and they offered me a swig of their beer. I accepted and one asked, "How is your day?" I said, "Great, but my knees are starting to give out." He answer-ed, "Yeah me too." Then he told me his age, 47, and I told him I was 61, he practically fell out of the chair in shock. We bonded momentarily as fellow mountain sliders with aching knees. There is a saying people admonish me with these days, 'You are only as old as you feel.' That is often meant to encourage older people to keep a youthful attitude. Oh yeah, unfortunately, sometimes I think young and the body still aches and hurts and feels old.

I look for wisdom in the inevitable changes of aging. Wisdom comes from knowledge and experience intelligently applied with heart. Wisdom provides fuel to get through rough patches in the aging Boomer. Days when the body is stiff in the wrong places, days when the knees ache. Those are the days when the wise older person practices awareness and enjoys simply carving turns on the slope, not jumping fifty feet off the cornice.

After connecting with the mountain and its denizens, I stopped for a cup of coffee at the local grind in the village. Spying a book rack that said, 'Support your local artists,' I opened a poetry book written by a retired fire captain and felt an instant kinship. Com-munity takes many forms, from the Zulu chorus to the achy- knee skiers to the village poet. Recognizing the narrowing of life that often comes with aging, it is my practice to regularly break out of routine, breathe in, and then give myself a pat on the back when it is done. I treasure those moments of a vital, vibrant, and engaged life. Not necessarily a youthful life, but a life that is fully alive.

Inner Journey:

☐ Identify communities of common interests or values in your life. How do you feel about the people?

☐ After you quit a fulltime job, how did you see your world narrowing?

Action Steps:

☐ Sample new groups or activities. When you find a likely fit attend regularly for at least a month.

☐ Recall a sport or other activity because you felt you were getting to old to do and you dropped (basketball, tennis, night clubbing). Perhaps find an adjustment, and renew that interest?

Chapter 34
Taylor Camp: Free Expression in Community

The great challenge of adulthood is holding on to your idealism, after you lose your innocence.
—Bruce Springsteen

If we keep our little flame alive, our first feeling of enthusiasm of who we are, without the influence or intervention of others, we will prevail.
—Patti Smith

One morning I walked into one of my local non-corporate coffee-houses, deep in thought, fully intending to hunker down and work on my book. A mix of millennials and Boomers were hunched over their laptops fervently doing status updates. Then I saw a friend focusing on his project in the prime window space. After I settled into a spot in the other room, this character came over. We proceeded to dive into a conversation that led to the Big Q that has been dogging me: The meaning of life, of my life, and the world. We are similar in age and, like me, he has forged a new mission after a traditional job/career. He works daily on a mathematical formula that explains the laws of the universe. We engaged in an hour-long conversation on his theories. Then I asked him point blank, "Joe, what is your purpose in writing this paper?" He flubbed around and finally said, "I need to do it."

Believing that there are no accidents and each path offers value if we can see it, I realized that our conversation led to my dominant question those days: "How do we find meaning in life and sustain it, after we have experienced fifty or sixty years and the inevitable disappointments and reality checks?" The topic had been taunting me for a couple weeks. It rose to the surface again another day, when the manager of a B & B in Maui mentioned a recent documentary film about Taylor Camp, a 'back to nature' commune in Kauai, Hawaii in the '70's. Memories about my first time in Hawaii poured in.

In 1976, I accidentally happened upon Taylor Camp while driving around Kauai in a rented camper with my girlfriend, Barabara. We had escaped to paradise, in love, and free of jobs, school, and home—We had found heaven on earth. The inhabitants welcomed us into their feast and celebration, even though we were complete strangers. We were of the 'tribe'—young people looking for an alternative to the disillusion and hypocrisy of the post-hippie, post-Vietnam 1970's America. They shared home-grown dinner, lilikoi and vodka punch, and herb. The evening evolved into a big campfire celebration complete with singing, guitar playing, and drumming. Always a documenter, I made an audio recording of the free-form sing-along, and drum circle. When it ended, I purchased a large quantity of their home grown herbal products. I played that cassette once at home, but then it disappeared forever. Unfortunately, I also lost/forgot that joyous night of spontaneous celebration of life and family.

Fast forward about 35 years back to the B & B on Maui. The proprietor's comment woke me up, and, like Lazarus, I began walking toward this recovered memory. Slowly, I stumbled on an understanding of what this all means for me at this time of life. Today, I am as free as I was at 25, perhaps freer because the economics of the next month or year or decade are handled. I reflected on that moment at Taylor Camp and felt a deep, hidden yearning I have carried all these years. On the surface it may be nostalgia for youthful freedom from responsibility or perhaps the urge for community or belonging. But for me, it also represented a call to adventure of the unknown, the fresh, the novel and the uninhibited.

Many threads weave through this long-ago experience but for me they all point to the ultimate question, the one that most people have at some time in their lives and the one that my mathematician friend at the coffeehouse is tackling. What is this life all about? How can I hone my sense of purpose in life? And how do I enjoy the ride?

The answer is always personal. Eventually, we all form our own opinions and solutions. It may be in religion, work, pleasure, or family. At this stage of life, it seems more pressing since the aforementioned 'have to's' are eliminated and the time left is more limited. My mathematician friend asserted he finds meaning when "the inner self no long feels separate from its experience." That day at Taylor Camp back in the day was like a floodlight shining on my core sense of meaning . . . *free expression in community*.

Inner Journey:

☐ Recall a time when you happened upon a fun and exciting event. Did you jump in and participate? Or did you leave?

☐ What is your opinion about living simply in community? Does it repel or attract?

Action Steps:

☐ Retrace your 'lost' youth, and go to a place where you experienced a lot of fun commu-nity, and expression.

Chapter 35
Didgeridoo Exposes in the Baths

*Belonging begins with self-acceptance . . . Believing you are
enough is what gives you the courage to be authentic.*
                    —Brene Brown

*You are either giving others the gift of your openness or the
clench of your refusal.   —David Deida*

The low groan of the didgeridoo in the world-famous hot sulfur
baths perched on the edge of the continent punctuated a deep
quiet in the crowd. A few dozen inner voyagers were arrayed in
claw-footed bathtubs, on massage tables, in poured concrete
shallow tubs, and on the narrow ledges. Past the unisex changing
rooms and through a door were the indoor tubs. The room was
devoid of words and movement, while the prehistoric, indigenous
Australian dreamtime instrument weaved its magic on the crowd
of seekers. Human shapes were barely distinguishable as male or
female in the misty, impromptu meditation hall, but one could
see groups of two or three in motionless embrace in the water
and on the tables. Not a stitch of clothes, not a towel strategically
draped, and no one in authority—simply a gathering of humans. A
family for the moment, self-selected from the larger clan

staying at the famous institute dedicated to expansion and exploration of human potential. The sound of the didgeridoo's low growl and periods of silence highlighted the magic.

I went to *Esalen* to partake in the elixir of the waters and the land, with the overt agenda of taking a workshop by the renowned career counselor/shaman Rick Jarow of Vassar College. Encouraged and sometimes pushed by a friend to take the leap out of my 'been there, done that' mood of late, I found Esalen was right on time. Living in Ocean Park/Venice, CA, famous for its counter-culture and its cutting-edge spirituality, I easily slipped into the teacher's 'know-it-all' attitude after a career in public education. What could I possibly learn, and besides, I've listened to the book? When I called Dr. Jarow to check it out, he said, "It isn't the workshop or the data, it is the land and the waters that transform." I jumped in my car and headed to scenic Highway 1 and Big Sur.

From the moment of arrival with my friend, the Runner, I felt aligned and synchronistic. After checking in at the front office, Jarow appeared out of the misty hill, and I stuck out my hand without hesitation—"Greetings Rick, I am here." From then the flow was on, from the waters to the communal dining to 'chance' meetings on the trails or the baths.

It was a tough week and pushed my 'know-it-all' buttons occasionally, but many times sheer joy arose for no reason. Welcomed by a semi-permanent community of 200 students, who aged 20's to 70's, of all ethnicities, and a wide range of economic classes, I felt at home. My tribe was present and no longer hidden in the masses of my city home. Eventually, I smiled at each passing person and enjoyed the communal meals. Even if you're alone, it is hard to be lonely with this warm and friendly crowd.

Slowly I relaxed and realized my unconscious 'story': How can I say I am for community when I push away these open hearts? Bogus! In a moment of truth-telling with the co-facilitator of my workshop, I got that Esalen offered what I want. Now, can I say yes?

My class had an unusually large contingent from my section of Los Angeles—Santa Monica/Venice. That indicated to me that even in the big, anonymous city, I am not really alone. My tribe was there at Esalen and back home in the anonymous metropolis. A couple weeks before, I had met some of the tribe accidentally at Big Bear Lake and this week I met them en masse in Esalen. As someone said in the workshop, 'This is a good day to die.' My addendum: A good day to die to the old, isolated, anonymous self and see the friendly trees in this dense forest and the misty hot tubs.

Inner Journey:

☐ Recall a time at summer camp. Were you anxious? Friendly? Homesick? Excited?

Action Steps:

☐ Go to a retreat or seminar by yourself. Check your mood before it starts and then in the middle. Can you identify when the energy shifted?

☐ In your daily life make an effort to acknowledge people you find interesting.

Chapter 36
Your Tribe May Be Next Door

*A man travels the world over in search of what he needs
and returns home to find it.* —*George Moore*

*To be rooted is perhaps the most important and least
recognized need of the human soul.*
                    —*Simone Weil*

Seeking respite from the concrete jungle and cacophonous vibes
of Santa Monica, I got in in my car and rolled a mere twenty
minutes to my country redoubt. After racing through the
winding mountainous road of Topanga Canyon, I posted outside
the Waterlily Café (featuring hippie style stained-glass lettering)
in the cool air and bright sun. My short journey covered ten
miles and forty years of my life.

The air was fragrant with the scent of patchouli, while I surveyed
a rare scene. Posters advertised the upcoming Topanga Days festival with a roster of local and international bands. A guy walked
by in cowboy hat, another jumped in his old pickup truck. A
middle-aged couple dressed in black leather, spoke in Farsi, and
then jumped on their Harley. A small pop-up tent was pitched in
a corner of the parking lot next to yucca and cactus mixed among

the sage and palm trees. A 50-ish woman dressed in full horse riding regalia got out of her Lexus SUV. At the table next to me sat a young, bearded guy with big shells poking through his left and right ear lobes wearing hiking boots. His girlfriend was dressed in a floor length black skirt, black sweater, and charcoal scarf. A typical, eclectic Topanga crowd.

My thoughts drifted to a girl I dated many years ago, who lived in a trailer and kept the two horses she rode in the Canyon. Then I remembered a wild night listening to a local sixties boogie band, *Canned Heat,* at the long defunct *Topanga Corral.* I smiled with remembrance of the night our obstinate buddy refused to leave a party we had crashed 100 yards from this spot, the once-in-fifty years snowfall in the Canyon, a recent romantic night at the organic, creekside restaurant, *Inn of the Seventh Ray*, and finally, of yesterday when I attended the sixteenth annual Earth Day celebrations and purchased a red, gold, and green tie-dyed Tshirt.

Much water has flowed under the Topanga Creek Bridge, since those early days. I tend to obsess on how to bathe in the stream of life with **saudade** (Portuguese, translated roughly as yearn-ing for the past), without nostalgia and melancholy. In everyday life, we segment time with arbitrary beginnings and endings to organize what is actually a seamless whole. My drifting reverie was more than just nostalgia for the 'old days,' it also pulsed with an urgent spirit for more life these days.

Too often I've lived through my concepts and not fully in the ebb and flow of experiences, in spite of lip service to full express-ion in life. For many years, on vacations I wandered the world, from tropic isles to desert rocks, wooded spiritual retreats to urban chic, but this day I wandered next door. Like Voltaire's *Candide*, after many trips all over the world I am now back to the beginning. The freedom and peace and community I always sought were always right here, but my vision was occluded by familiarity.

The idea of tribe informed my world view as I moved into the elder years. In our generation, we identified and joined our tribe through certain markers: beads, incense, long hair and black-light posters on the wall. In our time of elderhood, we have a boon to offer the tribe. Within most of us lives the desire to gift our hard-earned wisdom, to not let the dream die with us, and to revive and renew our personal vision. What is your tribe? The wisdom you bear will be clear when you find them. Like mine, they may be next door in a neighboring canyon.

Inner Journey:

☐ Recall your home and friends of your youth, what were three prominent characteristics of those people?

☐ Was there a place that you visited regularly for fun? Bar, park, neighborhood?

Action Steps:

☐ If possible, go back to that place, and walk around and see what remain, and what has changed.

☐ What is a value from those days that you still hold? Visit a group or event on that topic.

Chapter 37
Build Bridges over Your Generation Gap

Keep an open heart. We are wired to find love.
—Helen Fisher

When you can't make up your mind between two even balanced courses of action, choose the bolder.
—William Joseph Slim

Prompted by a notion that popped in my head, I visited a neighborhood church, the Church in Ocean Park. Built in the 1920s, it has been a bastion of alternative cultural and progressive political events for the forty years I've lived in the area. In the entry way I saw a group of five holding hands and praying, a tall, long-haired young man and four young women dressed in yoga togs, calm and peaceful.

Upstairs the glow of the blacklight highlighting a fluores-cent paint mandala summoned old memories of concerts, black light posters, and head shops. The yoga class was finishing with a room of about 100 lying in savasana (corpse pose), deep in meditation. Mats were rolled and stowed and then we were ready to dance, the *Sacred Dance*.

On the pulpit festooned in Indian fabrics, dreadlocks, and prayer beads, an eclectric band of violin, didgeridoo, djembe' drums, guitars, and bass performed. Unfolding slowly and meditatively, the crowd of all ages and genders but mostly twenty, and thirty-something women awoke. The free-form and unconditional dance of individuals merged into a diaphanous body of twirling, jumping, gyrating oneness. Flowing sarongs covered whole-back tattoos, yoga pants, skintight tank tops, and handwoven vests. Hair styles ranged from dreadlocks to waist length blonde to bald to gray to colored spikes.

It could have been 1970 and not 2012, except for one crucial element. Contrasted with the '70's, in this youth culture there was a sprinkling of older people. Individuals like me who were *in* such places in the 70s, but back in the day the old generation would have nothing to do with us and vice versa.

This segment of the youth today has taken the torch handed to them by the original hippie generation (yoga, meditation, free dance) and improved on it with greater ethnic and musical diversity. On stage, the performers were a mix of ethnicities and played a mix of world beats, folk melodies, and Hindu chants. Beyond all the apparent differences there was a celebration of oneness.

Walking into that setting with my 1970 ideas, I feared that they might not be cool with an older guy in their party. Not at all. By the second thirty-minute song I jumped and contact-danced with the best of them. In keeping with the theme of unity in the many, a giant circle formed to close the night and each dancer said their name, no longer anonymous consumers of a performance but members of a group—the *Sacred Dance.*

I learned that night:
1. **The generation gap has bridges.**
2. **The seeds of love the hippie generation planted have bloomed**.
3. **Movement liberates the spirit**.

The *Sacred Dance* had been on my 'to do' list for months. Each month something pressing kept me away, the undone taxes due next week, the emails unanswered, the dishes not washed, or most crucially the Lakers on TV. I always had a case for staying home—the default position for most people in the evening, especially those over fifty. Breaking out of that inertia and into active life took effort. Without effort I would have been sitting like a stiff on the couch with a glass of champagne or two. I balanced trusting the inner call and making right effort. That night I got off the couch and in the flow.

What a great ride. It confirmed again for me the kids are alright. The generations are not at war like back in my youth. I know many people in their twenties and thirties who are fun to be with and enjoy my company. One fellow, Evan, I met at the coffeeshop. He considers me a peer even though he is thirty years my junior. He said, "It is what is in the heart that matters, not age." This young man has many tribal tattoos, piercings, and earns his living on his computer.

Renewing, reviving, and reinventing Boomers can learn a lot from the young people today. Among my new activigties, a yoga festival, Earth Day celebrations, Facebook groups of mixed ages, and get out and do something new and different. I am not afraid to stand out. With luck, I am considered a wise elder. Regardless, I enjoy the sweet fruit of the seeds *we* planted then. You too will probably find it rather familiar.

Inner Journey:

☐ Recall a concert, demonstration, party back in your twenties. Were you free or inhibited? Belonging or separate? Happy or anxious?

Action Steps:

☐ Go to a yoga/kirtan festival, a Burning man event, wine bar, or anything new.

☐ Advanced level: Attend a new activity dressed in the typical regalia of the crowd.

'You Don't Need Help from Anyone Else,
Express Yourself'
—Charles Wright/Watts 103 St Rhythm Band
(Wright)

PART 7.
CREATIVITY AND EXPRESSION

Chapter 38
Kooks and Creativity

Do not be too timid and squeamish about your actions.
All life is an experiment. —*Ralph Waldo Emerson*

Letting go gives us freedom, and freedom is the only
condition for happiness. —*Thich Nhat Hanh*

At a well known Southern California surf beach, a new costume
was draped on a local statue that depicts a surfer riding a wave.
Overnight pranksters built a papier mache' shark's mouth engulf-
ing the surfer. The statue strikes a pose that is inimical for a
good surfer and is mocked by locals as the *Cardiff Kook*. Soon
after being erected a few years ago a series of such pranks were
per-petrated on this community landmark. Over the years it has
been covered with costumes from clown to female stripper.

Kook is surfer slang usually used as the ultimate putdown.
Writer and surfer Peter Heller wears that label proudly and
states, "Being a kook is a way of life. It's about being willing to
learn something new, to make a fool of yourself and just
go for it." The Cardiff Kook pranks express the freedom to try
on different personae and just go for it in public. The Kook

regularly attracts the local media with regular TV reports it gets praise from passersby and surfers alike. When dressed, by pranksters most celebrate it. The Kook is fun for the community.

I learned valuable lessons about creativity from this oddity. When I began practicing the creative arts, I noted my tendency to resist trying the new, out-of-type activity. Holding back, or worse, giving half effort short-circuited the fun of creativity. And as an older beginning artist, I had up a lot of excuses to not 'go for it.' My inner criticisms included, the learning curve is too steep, I am not talented, and who cares if I do it? Each of these cop outs are eschewed by the Cardiff Kook. Which is a lesson for all.

Lesson 1: His kook-ness is proudly displayed and loved by the community. *Being a beginner is not necessarily going to face public approbation.*

Lesson 2: The prankster(s) gives him a variety of roles to try on. *Experiment with new and personal approaches to the new art.*

Lesson 3: Public acclaim and interest accrue to the kook's costumes. *Sometimes the different, unusual, and original are enjoyed by others.*

Creativity can and often is fun. The prankster and the *Cardiff Kook* are great exemplars of the courage it takes to practice creative expression. Especially for those who were told at a young age, like me, that we couldn't draw or sing or act. The idea is just do it, do your thing, **express yourself**. The attitude we bring to the art is more important than any talent we may think you don't have. Sure, there may be a long period of skill development. And yes, sometimes I may be a 'kook.' The world may be waiting for the kind of kookiness we share. And besides, the Kook has some cool costumes.

Inner Journey:

☐ When did you intentionally do something really wacky and out of character?

☐ Imagine wearing some outlandish costume, not a character but wild or kinky.

Action Steps:

☐ Go to an event where wild and freaky behavior prevail—Burning Man, Venice Beach, masquerade party.

☐ In public do or wear something you would normally consider crazy or out of your normal zone.

Chapter 39
Turn Fantasies to Realities

We all have dreams. But in order to make dreams come into reality, it takes an awful lot of determination, dedication, self-discipline, and effort.
                    —*Jesse Owens*

Keep away from people who try to belittle your ambitions. Small people always do that, but the really great make you feel that you too, can become great.
                    —*Mark Twain*

Last week I met a former acquaintance at the local writer's café. He had just returned from the UK and was ready to roll out his new documentary film. Our conversation sparked some exciting ideas for promoting the film around the country. The plan sounded good but before committing to a supporting role in the project, I deferred and requested time out to reflect on it. A day later while soaking in my backyard hot tub, a nub of doubt arose around my desire to be the principal or partner in a project, not an assistant. I was a loyal employee for almost thirty years, and when the boss said jump, I said "How high?" So I had a serious case of 'been there, done that.' Digging down to the marrow, I found an answer. *I have a dream and that is what I need to do. Time is running out.*

Moving into new passions, activities, and work in the next chapter challenges most people on many levels. At its base creativity is essentially taking authorship of one's life. True creativity comes from the inside out. A natural flow of energy may happen in conducive settings, but the deeper genesis lies within the individual's own soul. At times my inner guidance gets rusty, since we are socialized to be productive and achieve things such as jobs, money, or even travel destinations. For me, the spark plug to creating begins with meditation. And frequently ideas arise and sometimes not.

After letting an issue or challenge simmer for awhile, usually I get a glimmer of an insight or solution. Then I practice a technique I learned in my role as a manager of teachers, *if it isn't in writing it did not happen*. The ideas, plans, goals, and strategies that I commit to I write in some form, in essays, in a poem, and in 'to do' lists that I post around the house. With writing there is clarification and commitment. My next step for action on a big rock or challenge is sharing it with a trusted friend or colleague, someone who understands my work and supports the mission. Often during that discussion further honing of the vision emerges.

A potential pitfall for me is our American ethos of rugged individualism. Yes, it is satisfying to grow your own passion, be it a new business or a new artistic expression, but without support and assistance I find it more difficult and maybe impossible. For years, I thought of writing a book and then in the midst of a creative spurt my girlfriend said, 'Hey put together a book!' I began by writing a description of it and then discussed it with trusted friends. The vision and friends encouraged and sustained me through the details and tedium of editing, compiling, and formatting. I carried it through to completion and gained the immeasurable gratification of accomplishment. Of course, when that door closed, then many more opened, such as going to open mikes and reading the pieces, posting on line and so forth. Support kept me accountable.

Perhaps you are one of those supremely gifted and determined persons who can succeed by going it alone, and it works for you. Most people when they get to the third chapter or retirement have spent forty years following orders and fitting into systems at work and society. Consequently, they may be a bit out of practice with what psychologists call the inner locus of control. Activating and developing new passions or friends can be daunting on many levels later in life. Often it is the reason people stay in jobs they no longer enjoy or stay in hobbies they have done since high school, and get bored, burned out, or cynical. I needed courage to step into the new and keep with it through the learning curve and reap the joy of living the dream.

Most of us have a fantasy project in the dark recesses of the mind. Something you have long thought about but not done. Perhaps it is writing a book, the most common goal according to the website, *43 Goals*. Or maybe it is learning guitar (also in the top 5) or traveling to Australia? What will it take to get in motion? Taking action, the fantasy becomes a dream and the dream is possible. And if not achieved, at least you will have the satisfaction of knowing that you tried. I hate it when fantasies linger and clutter my mind. Free up space on your inner hard drive with action and then find satisfaction.

Now, I'm looking for my next dream or book project.

Inner Journey:

☐ Spend some time meditating on and remembering your dreams. What would you like to be, do, and have in the domains of home, relationships, work, and health?

☐ Write out a sense-rich description of each of those dreams. Include such things as physical description and feelings it would evoke in you.

Action Steps:

☐ Make a list of next physical things to be done in working on that dream. Develop a timeline of what you want to accomplish in six months.

☐ Just begin with some action today.

Chapter 40
Leap BEFORE YOU Look

When you cannot make up your mind between two evenly balanced courses of action, choose the bolder.
—William Joseph Slim

Character cannot be developed in ease and quiet. Only through experience of trial and suffering can the soul be strengthened, ambition inspired, and success achieved.
—Helen Keller

On a recent hot, summer, weekday night, I hung out with an eclectic group in some unusual ways. Simultaneously, the TV was playing a yoga video, a guy was singing with a karaoke mike, and a group nibbling on the raw, organic, vegan fare.gathered in a corner in earnest conversation. After integrating myself with some casual conversation, I settled in to enjoy the festivities. In my experience of partying over many decades, parties generally are of two types, loud music and dancing or conversational.

On this night I encountered a twenty-first century party with today's young generation. An entertainment revue was about to begin. First, a young, fit guy got on the floor and portrayed Beyonce's writhing to a tee, then a chubby guy with his hair in a sumo wrestler knot tore off his shirt and simulated sex with the Beyonce impersonator. They were followed by a super athletic dude in a re-creation of his not so distance high school break-dancing days. Everyone was encouraged to jump up and show their stuff in the center. All received great applause.

I was invited to this party of twenty-somethings by a young acquaintance. My first reaction when he invited me was to beg off. After all, he is much younger than me. Besides what kind of a party is happening on Monday night. I have to get home to watch MSNBC after my regular meditation group meeting. I noticed as I considered going that I had a host of excuses to stay in my narrow, comfortable routine. I could have sat on my recliner and imagined what I missed, but I would have been way off-base. I pushed off the shore of my safe harbor and dipped my big toe in the water of the party.

Caution, planning, and research all have their place in building a new life after retirement, but one element that gets little attention is the *comfort zone*. By the time one retires, he/she has filled and emotional debris basin with detritus from a wide range of experiences 'good' and 'bad.' Wary of the unknown, many keep it safe and choose not go out to new places or make friends or learn new avocations. Security and routine have their place, but when they become the only place boredom ensues. Novelty excites and elevates the spirit.

Remember the first time you saw the Grand Canyon or fell in love? Very different events, but they both provide the excitement of the unknown. Craving newness, I quit tennis, my primary sport since youth due to physical challenges. And now I experiment with new sports such as badminton, table tennis and SUP. Put out-dated and unfulfilling habits in the dustbin of your history. Take a stand for the new and fresh. My mother practices this attitude. Since retiring she has learned a variety of painting styles, sculpture, and Sudoku.

I have not off-loaded everything tried and true. I have an old friend from high school who says he doesn't want new friends. He doesn't have to feel the anxiety of the unknown. I say keep the old friends, if there is still juice. But by reaching out for new friends and activities, there is an advantage. We tap the rich vein of new experiences. Learning new activities stimulates the brain and is recommended to stave off age-related Alzheimer's, depression, and myriad other age-associated conditions

When I am invited to something new, rather than defer to the predictable and comfortable, if I can fit it in my schedule, I say *yes*. Maybe I'll patronize a new place, call new acquaintances, attend a creativity session, paint a picture, or take a class. All of these are adventures into the novel. If it is a tossup, I just say yes. I open the door for the magic of the unknown to manifest. Is it always good, successful, or fun? Absolutely not. I recall a recent trip to a beautiful Caribbean island in the off-season that was a major letdown. Not much to do and very few fellow tourists, but I did gain a friend in Australia with whom I am in regular contact. And I learned that Tobago is the only place in the world where they hold annual goat races in a brand new stadium.

Facing the third chapter is my impetus to **Leap before Looking.** Don't just think about it, do it. Who will be there? Can't predict. What will happen? The unexpected. And if it turns out to be a mistake, at the very least I got in motion. Pushing into the unknown prevents plaque of the emotional arteries and keeps the energy flowing. Ride that flow to adventure. Time is getting shorter, the body is getting more aches, and the bucket list of life is waiting. Just Leap and then Look back and smile.

Inner Journey:

☐ Reflect on your life and consider actions you did NOT take and the results. In honesty, do you have any regrets that you did not at least try?

☐ Imagine your near future and something you have long considered doing. What considerations come up around that?

Action Steps:

☐ Today do something completely without planning or analyzing. For example, select the first item on a menu, or go to the first restaurant that pops into your mind. Evaluate the experience afterwards on ease or not.

☐ Stretch a bit and sign up and attend a brand new activity or sport. (Be sure to give it time to grow on you.)

Chapter 41
Meaning of Life? Create It!

The more sand that has escaped from the hourglass of our life, the clearer we should see through it.
—Jean Paul Sartre

Art is man's constant effort to create for himself a different order of reality from that which is given him.
—Chinua Achebe

Staring out at the early morning sunrise, my mind is a blank slate. No specific problems of survival, relationship, or health crowding my thoughts. It hit me on a bright and cold winter morning. What if there is no higher purpose? No mission. Nothing special to be done? No unique 'gift' to share—just living here and now with highs and lows and mostly 'in betweens.' Living in any way that is appropriate to the person, place, or time. What if this is it? No meaning of life, thus no heaven or hell. No reincarnation. No more SEARCHING high and low. Life give us enough of both.

Personally, I'm maxxed out. **Finally, I declare—'No more seeking ultimate meaning and purpose of life.' I finally get what Victor Frankl said in his classic *Man's Search for Meaning*—we each make up the meaning of life.** In essence, he asserted we are all artists who create our personal purpose or not. A recent teacher,

Don Miguel Ruiz, in the *Four Agreements* called this world 'the dream of the planet' and we are all the artists of our dream working on the canvas of our lives.

At the gym the other day, an acquaintance spontaneously offered his view of the afterlife: We don't die, we simply dissolve back into the earth, into the cosmos which is going nowhere from nowhere—no big bang with its beginning and implied ending. This guy is not a spiritual seeker, but he has lived life. In his late sixties, he works at a local lumber yard. Over the years he has re-galed me with tales of his youthful adventures running marijuana across the US/Mexico border, getting arrested, years of incarcera-tion, and jailhouse tattoos. Under his rough and crusty demeanor resides an artist. He draws and paints a wide range of subjects from nudes to lizards to landscapes. That is how he makes sense of it all. He makes art and that gives his life meaning.

'Retirement,' *freedom—'doing what I want when I want,' '*has not been at all like I expected. How I yearned for this endless vacation. Eventually after leaving the job, I felt adrift, like the legend of the Flying Dutchman condemned to wander aimlessly for eternity. I sought something to attach meaning to—a woman, a job, a new title. I was Ulysses trying to get home and taking many unproduc-tive detours—complete with tempting Sirens and devouring Cyclops—in my quest for meaning and purpose. It took years to see that the answer is in me. It reminds me of how released pris-oners often find a way to return. It isn't necessarily self-destruc-tion; it is a return to the known, predictable, and manageable.

Spiritual teachers often say self-*less* service brings meaning, because giving satisfies, fulfills, and adds meaning to life. My quest for right service (purpose?) felt like the arc of the cov-enant. Does it exist? I volunteered a lot when I was working.

But finding a good fit after work has vexed me. A litany of questions arose with each possibility: Can I learn and grow? Is it fun? Will I be around agreeable colleagues? Will my skill-set be utilized? Is it 'meaningful?' And finally, will I be free to 'innovate?' In my former profession, they described me as being 'innovative' with eyebrows raised. Nowadays I don't have to kowtow.

Then I got it: Service for me must include creativity—self-expression! Creating challenges awakens me. It also brings up unknown issues and memories, but I know when I put fingers to keyboard or brush to canvas, I am liberated. Sometimes it is too much and I feel overwhelmed and I have to escape to travel, relationships, entertainment, or mood-altering substances, but the vibe doesn't go away. When I do face the blank canvas, the computer screen, or any creative activity, freedom beckons.

That is where I find meaning—in the *Creative*. 'Retirement' is an ideal time to allow the creative spirit to flourish—no boss to please, nothing to prove, just real, personal expression. If I can do it, anyone can. Bereft of 'natural' talent, still I've had painting exhibits, poetry readings, published articles, and studied guitar, drum, and dance. Although sometimes torturous, the creative act manifests my uniqueness. And that is contentment and meaningful—to me.

When I feel something missing and seek meaning, I jump into the water of the *Creative* and like Ulysses ride my lifeboat into wild storms, smooth waves, and find satisfaction.

Inner Journey:

☐ Consider how much time and energy you have spent trying to figure out your purpose, your calling, or your mission. Write a paragraph on the merits of that search and what you have learned about yourself.

☐ Take the time to dream of something that calls you. It could be a location, a person, a job, or a possession.

Action Steps:

☐ On the above item, what is the very next action step? Research doesn't count. After the research what is to be done (physically) to make it happen?

☐ Write it down where you can see it every day— under a magnet on the refrigerator or a white board in your office.

Chapter 42
The Key to Creativity:
Repetition + Expression

**Spend Too Much Time in the Tavern and
You'll Have a Hangover!**

*Ever tried. Ever failed. No matter. Try again. Fail again.
Fail better.* —*Samuel Beckett*

*Sometimes you have to play a long time to be able to play
like yourself.* —*Miles Davis*

One week, bookended by a beginning guitar class at McCabe's
Guitar Shop in Santa Monica, CA and a painting retreat at the
Community Center of Encino, CA, I was buffeted by a common
challenge of the reinventing Boomer—learning new difficult skills.
Guitar classes were held in a room that does triple duty as
concert hall, classroom, and showroom. All types of stringed
instruments ranging from ukulele to classic Fender electric guitars
to hand-made mandolins filled the walls. The classes are packed
full with instruction on technique and practice drills. In contrast,
Master Rassouli's (a world famous painter and founder of the
Fusionart school) painting retreat, the opposite approach was
taken, no technique—*nada*. His approach seeks to inspire free
expression. Taught in an empty, cavernous, multi-purpose
hall, the room fits his method perfectly.

Each class stretched me. The guitar class pushed me beyond my capacities to absorb new skills with the chord changes, fingering, and timing of the guitar. I ended up getting more and more frustrated by the minute. Finally, I just shut down and stared at the sheet music, unable to move my hands. On the other hand, prepared to paint another masterpiece with Rassouli, with new canvas, new brushes, and ample acrylics, I spent the day bobbing around like a castaway's bottle in the sea with no direction or achievement. Between these polar opposites is the sweet spot of growth/learning in the creative arts.

Experiences in the arts offer the satisfaction of pursuing dreams creativity postponed during the work years. It may be playing a musical instrument, learning to draw or paint, writing a novel, or learning to dance. Throughout life people often pursue the arts as a way of self-expression and achievement. The big elephant in the room is that learning an artistic craft is tedious, slow, and often difficult, with a steep learning curve before ease much less mastery.

Joe Robinson (the author of an insightful book on leisure skills, *Don't Miss Your Life*) reminds us of the work of play, 'It Don't Come Easy.' When you have no natural talent for the field but always thought it would be cool to play piano (or guitar or draw portraits or tango), it takes major motivation and/or passion to continue on past the unavoidable beginners' stage. This has a corollary in meditation practice, where a popular maxim is 'zen mind, beginner mind.' In that cosmology the highest place to be is a beginner. The beginner mind expresses freshness and joy in pure experience. But soon in meditation and in art one desires skill development and achievement.

Artistic pursuits are often seen as expression outlets for the soul. Indeed, I have experienced great liberation through creative expression. I had an art show a couple years ago called, *Expression as Liberation.* The rush from expressing oneself is liberating and fun, but it is also fleeting. You always come down. Kind of like an intoxication that wears off the next day, if we are lucky enough to not have a hangover. To sustain the high or the liberation one must keep taking more of the intoxicant, but in artistic pursuits the high fades without craft or skill development. The satisfaction of achievement is lacking.

Instructors of creativity such as Rassouli, open a door that can liberate the creative self. I recall my first long medita-tion retreat with noted American Buddhist meditation teacher Joseph Goldstein. My consciousness was so fresh and clear from ten days of meditation, the material world seemed to sparkle like Christmas lights, and every conversation was loaded with luminosity. And it felt permanent. He closed the retreat by warning us that meditation at home is often not fun, but filled with discursive thoughts and irritations that may keep one off the meditation cushion. He advised, "Just do it." Often after many years the practitioner benefits from a calmer, more focused mind and life, but the rough seas of practice must be traversed.

In art, the 'high' of flow or engagement in the moment excites but to keep getting that high one must slog through the tedious terrain of building skills often through tedious drills. An outstanding spoken word artist, Adwin David Brown says it this way, "repetition, repetition, repetition, and then flow.' The bliss of spontaneous creativity comes after many hours on the free throw line at the gym, drilling forehands with a practice partner, and swinging in the batting cage. Miles Davis, the master improviser, said he practiced the scales every day.

When we enter adulthood, we are fresh and open to learn new stuff, so the long hours of repetition are not so daunting. Brain scientists have determined that the human brain is not fully formed until around 28. After that we have filled in the empty spaces of our brain. We have to retrain part of our minds to learn the new skills and that takes more effort.

Deep satisfaction from creative practice comes with patience and a carefully designed plan for sustaining the growth. The quick high of untrained expression can be as ephemeral as last night's drunk. My personal mantra on climbing this mountain in the later adulthood is: Show up, be mindful and 'just do it,' (over and over and over again). And enjoy the routine.

Inner Journey:

☐ What kind of instruction do you prefer?

☐ Recall times of failure at learning a new skill. Did you persist until success?

Action Steps:

☐ Sign up for a class in a musical instrument that you've always wanted to play, or a dance, or a language. Attend for at least ten sessions.

Chapter 43
Achievement for the Fun of It

Nothing can add more power to your life concentrating all your energies on a limited set of targets.
                                    —*Nido Qubein*

The artist is one who wants to leave behind a gift.
                                    —*Otto Rank*

At my local non-chain coffeehouse, there is a man in his sixties who reports to 'work' every day, Monday through Sunday and intently scribbles equations with pencil and calculator. He prefers a table near the window because of the light. He arrives every morning around 8 am, goes home for lunch, and returns for the afternoon shift. He works on a big question: the ultimate meaning and interrelationship of everything in the universe.

After he completes the calculations, he enters it into digital form at home. Even though he does not have a PhD, he is intent on achieving his goal of publishing this paper in a respected scientific journal. He does not seek fame, he has no academic credentials to burnish, and he doesn't expect any financial return on the effort. The main purpose of his work is the work itself or pure achievement. In our many long discussions about his calculations and theory, I learned that he has had this 'calling' since high school days and now he has the time to pursue it.

Another friend and former colleague retired to a small town in eastern Virginia, after a long and successful career as a math teacher in the Los Angeles school district. For awhile he chauffeured his kids around bucolic hill country and worked part-time at his gym. But eventually boredom set in, and with the encouragement of a political science professor, he started an online journal (www.politicsandphilosophy.com). He made friends with academics in his area, he gave talks on his theories to graduate classes. Emboldened, he published an academic tome entitled *'What Can I Do'?* In it he exhorted readers to make a difference in the world through ethical choices. Before retiring, this fellow was only motivated by the bottom line, 'What's in it for me?' He never worked after school if he wasn't getting paid. Now, he works diligently to research, write, and publish a highly esoteric book. His motive? Share his accrued wisdom and insights on how to achieve social change.

After 'retiring,' a new life begins. Some individuals look at this time solely as well-deserved rest and recreation after years of labor. For others, it is a grand opportunity, 50–60 hours per week to fill in with exciting, intrinsically rewarding experiences. How can we make the most of this time while we still have health and energy? Martin Seligman of Penn State recently published *Flourish: A Visionary New Understanding of Happiness and Well-being,* his new theory of well-being. He defines well being with five dimensions; **Pleasurable** emotions, **Engagement** or passion, **Relationships**/community, **Meaning** or purpose, and **Achievement**.

I consider his formula not a prescription of a successful retirement but as an aspiration for life satisfaction at any age. The five elements don't have to occur in one activity, but wholistically over one's life. The only plans most retirees make at gold watch time are a list of all the fun things they are going to do now that they have time. I had this attitude, and it lasted about a year. Gnawing questions appeared—What is my life about now? Why am I not happy? What do I really want to do? What is my legacy? Where is my internal compass?

Leaving the job world at age 57 felt like graduating from college with similar questions: What am I going to do with the rest of my life? The good life as presented in TV commercials is to consume stuff and seek pleasure, whether it is a fancy car, trophy mate, or tropical vacation—extrinsic orientation. We're supposed to leave achievement behind after retirement and simply float downstream to the mouth of the river until we join the ocean of the departed. The two friends mentioned above chanced on an important facet of a flourishing retired life: **Achievement for its own sake**—intrinsic rewards. And as we all know, success takes work.

Inner Journey:

☐ What have you always wanted to learn but didn't have the time?

☐ Investigate ways of learning or doing and make a plan with a due date.

Action Steps:

☐ Now, do the next step and find a confederate to hold you accountable.

☐ Check & record your efforts. Set up the next action step and due date.

'Be Sure to Wear Flowers in Your Hair'
—Scott MacKenzie (Adler & Phillips)

PART 8.
BOOMER IDEALS,
REMEMBRANCE

Chapter 44
Remembrance, Not Nostalgia

We cannot teach people anything, we can only help them to discover it within themselves.
—Galileo Galilei

The secret of a good memory is attention, and attention to a subject depends upon our interest in it. We rarely forget that which has made a deep impression on our minds.
—Tryon Edwards

In the early post-retirement days, with more time available, I rummaged through some old keepsakes from my teens and twenties. I had thrown letters, reports, awards, recommendations, birthday cards, and journals into a cardboard box, and stored in the attic for many years. I was looking for some old sports equipment and discovered mice had feasted on my treasured artifacts. Salvaging the majority of them, I decided to put the stuff in a plastic carton to protect them. In the process of repacking the patched bell-bottom jeans and the Morrocan jelaba, I read my letters, journals, and unpublished essays. It was a time capsule, of qualities and ideals of my younger self.

In some ways, it affirmed that my current personality and values are very similar over the course of nearly fifty years, yet at the same time I noticed significant inner growth. Finding those fragments of my earlier self inspired me to reflect on the old days, hoping to not fall into a 'good old days' syndrome. With the clarity of hindsight and age, I read and rediscovered the rich ore of my timeless self. My past came alive and sparked some new ideas for changes in my present life.

I found a Pink Floyd poster, which transported me to forty years ago. It was my youthful time of exploration and freedom, when I was open and curious about new music, new places, and new people. One night while attending UC Berkeley, I recalled a concert that blew away my teenage innocence. I hadn't heard of Pink Floyd, but they had critical acclaim. A couple of friends and I jumped in my old Buick station wagon and rolled across the bridge to San Rafael and discovered a hippie fantasyland in a converted bowling alley turned concert hall named *Pepperland*. They had created a total environment painted in the style of the then current animated feature, '*Yellow Submarine*.' It was like going to another world. The Floyd's music escorted me and my cohorts into a colorful world of expression and freedom. We explored new musical and consciousness frontiers that night. Remembrance of the spirit of that early experience, beckoned me to lively up a bit in my current phase of life.

In the Sufi tradition they have a ritual called *zikr,* which means remembrance of god. They perform rituals intended to remember the true self, the unscarred self, the natural self who comes from a place of one with god. The practitioner seeks to recall that quality and *re-member*. That is to put the pieces back together in their original state. It is out of this remembrance that the individual aligns himself with love and the qualities usually attributed to the divine.

One opportunity of chronological maturity is **remembrance** of the past, but a pitfall is nostalgia. A memory may be about romance, youth, place, but it doesn't empower when one looks back with regret and missing the 'good old days.' Nostalgia may lead to depression and a litany of complaints about the world and one's self—'Back in those days people cared about each other' or 'when I was young, I had potential.' Nostalgia closes the door on life as it is now and lands one in the rocking chair telling tales of the good old days.

How do I practice **remembrance**, a positive re-membering of parts of one's self that have been lost in the fog of a long ago time? When memories emerge in thought, I don't push them away like a plate of tempting chocolate cake but invite it in. I welcome the recollection and become friends with it, and allow the old story to be a teacher about who I was, my ideals back in then, my dreams, passions, and the type of people I gravitated towards. The youthful self can speak with a deep wisdom of being and renew life and direction.

Remembrance for this Boomer has three steps:

1. Openness to cues and clues in my present life that refer to the youthful (often idealistic) self.
2. Follow that clue and see what qualities of life stand out.
3. Brainstorm or journal how to express that in my life now.

I perceive a clue by my emotional reaction to something. It may be a welling up of tears or perhaps a heightened curiosity or even a fantasy. I've learned to trust these insights and act on them. I follow up like a detective trying to crack a case. Then I research on the Internet, discuss with friends, free associate, or perhaps visit a relevant location, trusting the journey of life.

The trip of **remembrance,** or putting back together the lost or forgotten parts of the self into a new vision, an image grounded on the unchanging self takes effort. It isn't easy to find a path that satisfies your core needs of autonomy, belonging, and competence. But when I am on a mission of growth or step into the unknown, I find compatriots that align with core values, and then pursue progress and novelty in that direction. Similar to Pink Floyd that kind of trip may be the new adventure that makes the 'golden' years the most rewarding of life. And no drugs are needed.

Inner Journey:

☐ Close your eyes and remember some incident in your past. Pay attention to the scene including, smells, weather, environment, other people.

Action Steps:

☐ Contact someone you haven't seen for many years. Talk about the old days and your values back then.

Chapter 45
Them Changes

*If we don't change, we don't grow. If we don't grow,
we are not really living. Growth demands a temporary
surrender of security.* —Gail Sheehy

*We cannot live for ourselves alone. Our lives are
connected by a thousand invisible threads, and along
these sympathetic fibers, our actions run as causes and
return to us as results.* —Herman Melville

The spirit of the original hippie days knocked on my door at a
café on San Pablo Ave in Berkeley. While I sipped a dark roast
coffee, I gazed around this great 21st century café, with its fine
organic, fair-traded coffee, comfortable patio, classic knick-
knacks, and free wi-fi. An empty bottle of Lancer's circa 1966 sits
on a window sill. Surrounded by old stuff, the café evokes a
calmer, simpler time. But for many Boomers, the 60s and 70s,
didn't feel simple and calm.

The scent of cultural revolution was in the air. Our generation
was going to be different, anti-Establishment values informed us.
We wanted a change and we wanted it **now**. A prescient anthem
was Dylan's *'Times They Are A Changin'* (1962). Our frequent
protests resulted in some modest changes in the political sphere-

the lowering of the voting age, end of the draft, civil rights for women and so-called minorities and the impeachment of Nixon. But Buddy Miles reflected the stress of those times in his 1970 song, *'Them Changes.'* In other areas stewardship of the environment, ending futile and pointless wars, and economic fairness, we failed miserably. In these measures we have left our children a country in worse shape than we found it.

One of the most enduring gifts from the Boomer generation is the music and its corollary, the freedom to self express. Our music presented a vision of an idealized time of peace, love, freedom, and harmony in an actually highly contentious time. We pointed the middle finger at our elders who were 'square,' 'bigoted,' and 'uptight.' All things Establishment were at the risk of our ire and idealism. It was in the lyrics of the songs, but also seen in other forms of expression such as movies, clothes, and hair. We considered ourselves different, the **Now Generation** who would set about making the world right, peace and love. At the same time, there was a dark side, as at Altamont, when people were stabbed while Mick Jagger sang, *'Sympathy for the Devil.'* But many of us were dreamers and lived for freedom and love. Guided by John Lennon's words in *'Revolution,'* we sought to free minds instead of perpetrating violent revolution.

Following that guidance, we aspired to build a new society, but we failed. Our nation took a drastic turn to the right. Since Reagan's arms build-up that resulted in the implosion of the Soviet Union, we have been on a constant war footing. Coupled with excessive deregulation, anti-union policies, and tax breaks for the 1%, we now live with extreme natural disasters, climate change, increasing gap between the rich and the rest of us, self-righteous religious zealots, and never ending preemptive wars of aggression. It is no wonder that the youth of today look to our music for inspiration. We had great ideas and slogans but fell far short in achieving our vision.

In the 70's our generation, like others before it, was idealistic, but in the end our narcissism prevailed. The majority took the road most traveled and reaped the fruit of unsustainable lives. We Boomers have led the world to this point through the power of our numbers in the marketplace and the voting booth. Despite positive trends, such as expansion of gender and sexual equity, organic food, yoga, and electric cars, society has lost ground on key quality of life indicators, obesity, traffic, economic security, and personal privacy.

At a talk in Hawaii in 2011, renowned researcher on the science of human consciousness, Peter Russell, was asked if he had hope for the human race given the extremity of the challenges. His answer, "I don't know. I hope so, but I don't see the evidence for it." As I sat in that room of 100 Boomers and a handful of 21st-century yogis/hippies, I realized that a challenge of positive aging is to be knowledgeable, appreciative, and possibly aligned with one's past ideals.

Can we reconnect with our youthful vision of equal rights, economic justice, environmental sustainability, and the end of futile wars? But firstly, we need an honest inventory of our successes and failures. That recollection may be infused with regret or longing, but within the group memory is the power of community. Our generation once had hope, vision, and purpose. We can make a difference again. We now have the age and resources that come with it: time, economic freedom, knowledge, and mobility. Perhaps some will leave a positive legacy. To paraphrase Peter Fonda in *Easy Rider*, 'Let's *not* blow it again.'

Inner Journey:

☐ What do you miss from your youth? From your middle age (30–60)? What were your ideals in youth?

Action Steps:

☐ Pick one social issue that inspires your interest. How can you make a difference with your actions? Now do something concrete to address it.

Chapter 46
Going Back to the Truths of Youth

The aim of life is to live, and live means to be aware,
joyously, drunkenly, serenely, divinely aware.
—Henry Miller

In the depth of winter, I finally learned that within me there
lay an invincible summer. *—Albert Camus*

Sometimes going back is living in the here and now. I was invited to a showcase of a new friend's improv class, but inertia had me in its grip. I tend to be a stuck freak, comfortable with routine. Coaxed out by loyalty to my friend and desire to support, I jumped on my bicycle and rolled to the Promenade in Santa Monica. In a small theater in a back alley, I watched the class project of a dozen young people encased in bodies varying in age from 20 to 65. Each one took a turn at improvising on suggestions from the audience.

It takes courage to get up in front of an audience without a script. The older characters in the lineup practice my ideal, act young by opening to new experience. They practiced courage by digging a fresh well. In doing so, they shined a light on my definition of wisdom: *where experience meets heart.* Like the

Byrds once sung, it is no longer about how many toys (money/status) I have. In retirement many have the option to gather the lessons of life and join them with the curiosity of youth. And then ask, 'What's next? What can I bring to the party?'

As the largest generational cohort, we Boomers can still make a difference. We can revive youthful ideals of freedom, creativity, respecting nature, and community. But how do we temper our idealism of youth with the wisdom of maturity? What does it look like to be free? Can I live creatively? How can I best serve those in need? What can I do to preserve the natural environment?

Boomers were once known as the *Me Generation*, with the mottoes 'winners have more toys' and 'greed is good.' After the persistent economic and cultural insecurities of recent years, maybe it's time to reframe our generational image to the *We Generation*. We were once free and together. We cared about the world and life and expressed it in music, movies, and all the arts. We have so much more to give than to go off into the sunset quietly. A conference in Santa Fe, NM in 2012, *Navigating Your Future*, addressed this theme. When a friend informed me of this event, she added, "We're Not Done Yet." Maybe sixty is the new twenty.

Let's dust off those old dreams of a better world for you and me. I strive to recapture the spirit of hope and possibility of youth. Elderhood can be an odyssey of reviving or discovering that lost spirit and applying it to career/work, relationships/community, recreation/hobbies, social/political transformation, spiritual awakening.

A noted political scientist, Bill Pray, offers an approach to activating for social change in his recent book, *What Can I Do?*

In it he lays out a detailed strategy for personal empowerment that counters the current climate of aridity, insecurity, and cynicism.

Perhaps together we can summon the courage to work for the positive future we dreamed of. Why not join me for another wild and wonderful magical mystery trip. My overarching goal is to open to the unexpected thrill of painting a fresh canvas in this thing called life.

Inner Journey:

☐ What were some impactful places or songs
from your youth? Consider what message of
those songs stuck with you.

Action Steps:

☐ Go to or do something from back in the day.

☐ Find someone who is much younger than you
(15+ years) and relate the story of that exciting
event above and why it was.

Chapter 47

Step Back in the Old River and Taste the Fresh Water

The only real voyage of discovery consists of not seeking new landscapes but in having new eyes.
—Marcel Proust

I've been absolutely terrified every moment of my life and I've never let it keep me from doing a single thing that I wanted to do. *—Georgia O'Keefe*

The venerable maxim 'You never step in the same river twice,' popped into my mind as I drove south on Lincoln Blvd to LAX headed to a graduate seminar at a well-known personal growth organization—Landmark. Originally, I imagined a nostalgic trip to revisit a significant turning point in my life. At a non-nondescript office building I saw the first surprise of the night, the organization occupied a whole floor. I expected one room.

Escorted by a new friend from Australia, we went to the meeting room. It contained one hundred chairs arranged in a semi-circle facing the platform, with four white-boards and chalkboards that outlined the 'work' or agenda. Two high director's chairs completed the scene, almost a replica (except for the white boards) of the room where I did the original 'training' back in the seventies.

As before, the seminar leader began the evening by welcoming guests with a thumbnail description of the seminar. Well-dressed in a suit with an open collar shirt, he exemplified an educated, intelligent, and confident professional. Little had changed in this group in the over thirty years, since I last participated. In spite of name changes, retirement of its founder, his sale of the intellectual property, and myriad attacks in the mainstream media, the core of the training survived intact. More than I can say about my own body and spirit.

Although my seminar days are over, I was curious. My Australian friend had traveled over six thousand miles, to continue his work with this organization and to immerse himself in the rich stew of the consciousness/spiritual community of Santa Monica/ Venice. He was committed to reinvention. But I wondered why come so far? Initially, I had politely declined his invitation, not wanting to go through the high pressure sales pitch/enrollment process I remembered from the old days. Then at lunch one day he said with a big grin, 'You know mate, I forgot that as a graduate you are eligible to sit in on the seminar.'

Mulling it over, I decided that the time had come to revisit the origins of my personal spiritual path begun so many years ago—1979. I considered the *est* training the beginning of my personal/spiritual growth. My inner life awoke on those two weekends. Connections made after that first experience led to meeting an Indian guru and then a New Thought television minister. That first seminar led to a workshop which led to a retreat and many more. Personal and spiritual growth became a pillar of my life. Thirty years passed. I retired from my career in education. And touching base with significant places, persons, or events in my past, seemed like a pilgrimage.

Life review is common after significant transitions such as retirement. Where did I come from? What did I accomplish? When this friend invited me, my notion was that I would enjoy going down memory lane for an evening. Maybe like going to one's old high school or first summer camp. Remember the good things, and taste a bit of the old emotions. But subconsciously, I felt something needed to be completed. Some strings needed retying.

Sitting in that familiar setting and format, it felt like I had been on a long trip in space and returned to earth but time had stood still. I was older and maybe wiser, but the scene was the same. The chalk boards on the stage announced the intended results of the seminar and laid out the agenda for the evening. A highly verbal older woman reported she had been doing this work for over thirty years. She gave it credit for the three degrees she had earned, and declared her intention to publish her book, at last. A young woman shared her challenge in getting her new husband to understand her. Another person declaimed about her cranky neighbor.

The normalcy and common-sensical nature of their dilemmas struck me. Not in an obscure ivory tower way, nor in a dogma drenched church, but simply human and down to earth living: Real people with practical projects and goals in the world. The supportive and clear thinking of the seminar leader impressed me. He did not play around with platitudes and vague concepts. Real life, practical coaching.

In this highly transitory era where computers get updated daily and even the laws of physics are provisional, personal growth workshops have a short shelf life. In spite of the highly trendy nature of the human potential movement of the 70s somehow

Landmark has survived and prospered. Standing alone after all of its peers have long since died, Landmark (the successor to *est*) is over forty years old. Some of the old questions remain: Is it a cult? What's with the focus on enrollment?

My journey to the past showed me that the lessons I learned back in the day still apply and serve. My experience then was different, because I am different, but the message was the same. Tell the truth about your rackets, complete the past, keep your agreements, and live from intention. Timeless technology that works. The trip to the river that night was not a journey down memory lane, but a taste of the flow of my life.

Maybe some of my other experiences and education of years past are not dead and gone, but can be revived and applied in this stage of life. I like reconnecting with old programs, teachers, schools, places, and activities to see if there is still juice for me. The essence is the same and often refreshes me with its unique nectar.

Inner Journey:

☐ What made an impact on your personal growth in your youth? Do you still participate?

☐ Imagine a skill you wish you had learned back in the day. What are your feelings about that?

Action Steps:

☐ Visit some significant location or group in your personal history.

☐ Go to an activity or group you enjoyed years ago. Do you have any juice for it now?

Chapter 48
Shock, but No Awe at the Rose Parade

We are what we pretend to be, so we must be careful what we pretend to be.   *—Kurt Vonnegut*

Obstacles are those frightful things you see when you take your eyes of the goal.   *—Hannah More*

At the Rose Parade, 2011, among the prancing horses, the marching bands, the regal hand waving celebrities, and the cotton candy hawking vendors one of the dozen flower bedecked floats riveted my attention. A rumbling disquiet emerged from my core, a rumbling laden with protest. Visually the float was a typical mélange of flowers and papier mache, except not topped with dancing girls and erupting volcanoes, but packed with an explosive message. It depicted an old time railroad passenger car with a bunch of middle aged people smiling in anticipation of their destination. Emblazoned on the side was the name, Boomer Express 1946. My first thought was YES! Celebrate our generation of anti-war protest demonstrations, free love-in bacchanals, and social liberation. But alas, none of those impactful and well known markers of Boomers was recognized. In white (as in pushing up the daisies) flowers blared the terse and threatening phrase, *One in Eight*—sponsored by the *Alzheimer Association.*

Shock, anger, and chagrin bubbled up in my 61 year old mind. Are they hoping for donations by playing the fear card? Are they reminding us that the end is nearing, and it is not pleasant? After a lifetime busting age related stereotypes, do they think we are going to go down with an unconscious whimper?

I am quite aware of the passage of time and potential challenges that lie ahead. My Boomer express is not headed passively to the nursing home. That float was a wake-up call for me to express more fully with the rainbow of life's gifts, I got fired up with three Rs: **Remembrance, Recognition, and Revolution.**

Remembrance: Although portrayed as the Now Generation, the Boomers in the Sixties and Seventies referred back decades for stylistic cues in clothes (Victorian), posters (A. Beardsley), novels (Tolkien and Hesse), and politics (Karl Marx). These days, as we step into our last chapter, remembrance may mean another look at our values, dreams, goals, and spirit of our youth. Not slipping into morbid nostalgia, but tapped as a mother lode of energy for this stage of life.

Recognition: A key trait then was the willingness to expose and tell the truth about what was going on, rapping's original meaning. I reviewed some of my writing from high school and noticed how similar were the social and political issues then as today, from war to justice to the natural environment. Also, the personal values resonate today such as freedom, adventure, and community. Why not revive ourselves with more expression, community, and passion. No longer 20 or 30, but the core principles of youth remain at our core.

Revolution: Back in the day, we sparked revolutions in politics, relationships, music, art and just about everything else. A lot of those radical ideals were either co-opted or forgotten. Eventually, we grew up and settled down to the mundane aspects of life; work, family, house, and taxes. Today's graying formerly revolutionary cadre' has the potential of a wise soul with youthful passion. As we transition out of the narrow boundaries of thirty to forty years of responsible living, why not eschew the old-school concepts of old age with its mournful train to Alzheimers. With 21st Century technologies we can build community, share our wisdom, express freely, and foment a peaceful revolution.

To Alzheimer's Association and its float: Thanks for the reminder that time's awastin,' but I'm not riding that sorry train to Alzheimers. In my sixties, I stand tall, alive, unrepentant, and claiming my older age is a great age. Redemption is here and now, and it is there for those who still **remember, recognize,** and **revolt.** They *live the dream deferred*.

Inner Journey:

☐ Recall and write down the ideals you had for the world, your nation, and yourself, in the domains of,
   1. the natural world
   2. the political system
   3. your personal life

☐ With the wisdom of age, what are your ideals for above now?

Action Steps:

☐ Find and volunteer at an organization that seeks to improve one of the above.

☐ Set achievable and near term goals for yourself in that work.

'La La La Live for Today'
—The Grassroots (Julian, Mogull, & Shapiro)

PART 9.
ACCEPTANCE AND PURPOSE

Chapter 49

As the World Goes Global, Be True to Yourself

Have the courage to follow your heart and intuition. They somehow already know what you truly want to become. Everything else is secondary. —Steve Jobs

Be who you are and say what you feel, because those who mind don't matter and those who matter don't mind.
                    —Theodor Seuss Geisel

One afternoon on the beach in Sayulita, Mexico (near Puerto Vallarta), amid the horde of North American tourists drinking margaritas and eating ceviches, outnumbered by at least a few hundred beach hustlers to his one, I glimpsed a lone fisherman. He stood at the ready with net in hand, as the tide went out and the dozens of surfers rolled in. A young man in his thirties, he crouched among the tide pools as still as a statue and patiently studied each new wave ready to collect his dinner. Twenty years ago when I first visited this beach, his type was abundant. Just a few trailblazing surfers would have been on the waves.

So rare was this sight another gringo was also ready with his telephoto lens to film it. His patience proved greater than mine, and after ten minutes waiting for a catch, I continued my stroll through the palapas and vendors of cheap silver and hammocks. But the fisherman was not the only anomaly on the beach that day.

In a couple hundred yards, I saw a young girl adorned in tribal dreadlocks practicing her unique and strange craft. Not an ancient occupation like the fisherman's, but original to her. She wore a pointed wizard's hat made of bark, while weaving feathers and beads into jewelry. Not the mass produced hipster hats made in China that are the vogue today. Also, not making the typical colored thread bracelets made to order with your favorite sports teams, city, or someone's name. She was pursuing her path, her calling. Not following the throng of mass appeal.

These days in Sayulita the effects of globalization, with all of its ills and benefits stand out. A burgeoning Mexican middle class shares space with the North Americans now. Shopping at Costco, Home Depot, and organic farmers markets dressed in current styles, they are indistinguishable from the tourists until they speak. In part due to NAFTA, in part to modern communications, our cultures have blended into an amalgam of tastes and styles that serve the mass merchandising ethic. Middle-class lifestyles have an almost irresistible appeal all over the world with undeniable benefits of comfort and entertainment for millions.

Modern culture seduces. The message is clear: Drop traditional lifestyles and you too could be like the stars on the *telenovellas*. Only a few hold outs resolutely follow their inner calling, what comes natural to them, what is authentic. I met few here in this former sleepy surf beach, now a tourist friendly destination currently undergoing a major facelift of the old town center.

Following your inner call is never easy, but must be especially difficult in a town like Sayulita where the lure of the mass marketplace has arrived. I found another original on the beach named Xipatzin, a multi-talented musician, poet, and fire artist. He regaled me with his powerful 'Rumiesque' poetry instantly translated on the spot.

Be True to Yourself the Beach Boys sang in the Sixties. It heralded the emerging youth culture fifty years ago, when they wrote it. But being true to yourself is not an easy path. Many newly 'retired' persons find themselves lost, myself included. Freedom from the demands of 9 to 5 led to an existential dilemma for me. With a fresh canvas to fill, many questions arose; **What gives my life meaning? What do I want to achieve? What pleasurable hobbies/experiences call me? Who do I want to associate with? Where do I want to live?**

I was tempted to slip into default mode and pursue mass produced lifestyles, entertainments, and activities, designed to extract maximum dollars from me, the consumer. Bucking the system and living a personal path can be challenging to fishermen and crafts vendors on a tourist beach. They need to make a living. For new retirees like me, the challenge was to break out of my comfort zone and heed the innate urge and express my uniqueness. My motto: *Expression Is Liberation.*

A vision of an original and vital life guided my decisions after retiring, and fueled my quest to swim free from the homogenizing tide of globalization. Taking up the call to live from the inside out defines freedom for me. Even as the world around us changes. Why not be like the fisherman among the hawkers on the beach, like the girl weaving a kinky bark hat, and the musician doing didgeridoo healings on lobster red ladies from Montreal. As Robert Frost said back in the era when Beach Boys sang *Be True to Yourself*, taking the road less traveled makes all the difference.

Inner Journey:

☐ Scan your world (hobbies, work, home furnishing, sports, arts), and identify something that you have put your unique stamp on.

Action Steps:

☐ Next time you do that thing that is uniquely you, note it and congratulate yourself. If possible, share it.

☐ What have you been afraid to do because you aren't good at it? Do it anyway or sign up for lessons AND stay awhile.

Chapter 50
Coffee with Profits and Purpose

Our prime purpose in this life is to help others. And if you can't help them, at least don't hurt them.
                    —Dalai Lama

In nothing do men more nearly approach the gods than in doing good to their fellow men.
                    —Cicero Pro Ligario

Guided by GPS, I pulled into a mini-mall at the corner of Riverside Drand Congress in Austin, TX looking for a coffee shop named *Dominican Joe's*. I discovered it in an online directory. A fan of non-corporate coffee shops, I have three criteria for a place to make the top tier of coolness; 1) free wi-fi, 2) local events bulletin board, and 3) working ambience. The last is highly subjective and it's where personal taste comes in. For me, that usually means having comfortable couches, friendly staff, relative quiet, good light, patio, and at least a quarter of the patrons working with their computer screens. At *Dominican Joe's,* I encountered a wild card factor that catapulted that location to the top rank: **Profit with a greater purpose**.

Dominican Joe's was founded by a young graduate of the Univer- of Texas, who wanted to do something to make a difference.

While on a trip to the Dominican Republic, it hit her, *buy fair trade coffee directly from the farmers and open a coffee shop in Austin with a percentage of profits going to build and operate a school in the DR*. This came out in a chance conversation with the store manager, who was posting a flyer on the bulletin board. I already dug the place, because in spite of its location in a mini-mall, the place had a lot of soul, comfy couches, warm décor, and friendly staff.

On my road trip through the Southwest, I visited and imbibed at a wide variety of locally-owned coffee shops. Most serve a crucial function as a community center. In the historic area of Kingman, AZ, *Beale St Coffee* houses an avant-garde painting gallery. While I sipped my morning joe, a host of locals checked in for their morning coffee and gossip. At the *Santa Fe Baking Co*, a local radio program interviewed individuals on their projects. Being Santa Fe, NM, with its abundance of healers, artists, and environmentalists, their ten foot long bulletin board overflowed with flyers sticking out the edges. In Truth or Consequences, NM, *Little Sprouts* served more than double duty with an organic produce market, alternative healing products, and a deli counter. The absolutely coolest was the *Café Passe* on the super hip 4th Ave, Tucson, AZ. It functions as a hang-out, fine cuisine café, art gallery, and in the evening a live jazz venue.

But out of the couple dozen shops I sampled on this road trip, only two had an overt social agenda. The other is *Grace Coffee* in San Antonio, a beautiful bright room in a YMCA and owned and operated by a Christian church, staffed with jolly baristas and no tip jar. A sign announced its mission of using profits to serve the homeless— faith into action.

Starting in London a couple hundred years ago, coffee houses have always played an important role as gathering places for artists, intellectuals, and revolutionaries as well as neighborhood hang outs. Purpose through service is what distinguished *Dominican Joe's* and *Grace Coffee* and that is a reminder for us who have left the world of working for a living. Recent studies indicate that once economic sufficiency is reached, gratitude is what sustains happiness.

Service is an active form of expressing gratitude. It engages the soul and gives something beyond words, money, and time. It rewards the giver. Service often gives meaning to one's life. As we age, many of us need to feel relevant and service is a great way to contribute to the world. In fact, if we have achieved a comfortable life style in maturity, we did not do it alone. We all had assistance, from our teachers in college, encouragement from mentors, or simply the many hands who provided food and shelter. As Jefferson Airplane said back in the day, 'No man is an island, he is a peninsula.'

Giving back through service may develop into a life purpose. Psychologists have determined that older people with a purpose live longer and happier. My big take-away from this odyssey of coffee shops from Venice, CA to Austin, TX---Service can be the purpose that sustains a satisfying retirement.

Inner Journey:

☐ When have you given pure service? How was it?

☐ What were your childhood lessons about generosity of your time and money?

Action Steps:

☐ Brainstorm with a friend on new places and ways you could serve. Consider your avocational and professional interests. Do it!

Chapter 51

Ageless Spirits at the Bowl and in Life

Life's challenges are not supposed to paralyze you; they are supposed to help you discover who you are.
—*Bernice Johnson Reagon*

What do I have do to get out of doing these things twice.
—*Bob Dylan*

After a second round of drinks, a friend of more than forty years made a bland and pointed observation. He scored a solid hit, since I write about it, attend conferences on it, and read about it. He said, "You are obsessed with aging." "You may be right," I responded. His comments were sparked by my observation that most of the people in his Marina Del Rey apartment building are much older than us. I continued, "Being aware of where I am in life's time-line helps me to get on with it. Not waste time and make sure I live life full-out."

But that comment threw me into some reflection, 'Am I making too much of this aging thing? Is it coloring my approach to life?' Can I be present with aging and still be happy, vital, and hopeful? Age truly isn't everything. My greatest experiences in life are ageless; leaping the gorge at Victoria Falls (Zimbabwe), massive cascades at Iguasu Falls (Brazil, Argentina), sunrise at Haleakala Crater (Maui, Hawaii), and blue waters of Havasupai Falls (Grand Canyon, Arizona). And not to mention the thrills of personal relationships (fall in love at any age and feel young). And yet we often create separations in our life by age, and myriad other labels (ethnicity, class gender).

At the annual reggae night at the Hollywood Bowl in 2011, agelessness infused the air. Fifteen thousand people grooved as one in appreciation of the music and each other. Not limited by their human story which includes *age*, this community came together around common values expressed with a hypnotic beat and uplifting lyrics. There were young children, senior citizens, and many in between in the crowd. The artifacts of reggae culture, red, gold, and green apparel, could be seen on many. Even the performers spanned the stages of life from the 68 year old father of reggae, Toots Hibbert, who wrote the first song with reggae in the title, to Ziggy Marley, the son of Bob.

Singing and dancing to well known songs spread a sense of joy over the scene, we connected across the generations and grooved in the place where timeless spirit resides. I have attended outdoor reggae festivals for over thirty years, ever since the first Bob Marley day at MacArthur Park in downtown L.A. The one love vibration has been consistent at each, from *Reggae on the River* in Northern California to *Reggae in the Jungle* in Negril Beach, Jamaica to *Reggae Pon de Mountain* in Topanga, CA. All ages, community, and *upfullness* (positive vibrations).

I wonder how many places in life do we have that experience? Not at the typical church with ad-hoc racial segregation, not at work its status hierarchies, not at an evening on the town which breaks into sharply defined age strata, and even not often with our friendships. We self-segregate in so many ways.

Pushing against artificial, spirit limiting rules is my creed. Even as I accept and adjust to the changes that come with aging and changing life conditions, I ask---What can I do to be freer? How can I continue to enjoy sports even with my chronic bad back? What is a fun skill to learn? Can I re-imagine my life that express-es the openness, boldness, and curiosity of youth? At the same time, what adjustments do I need to make? Our essence may be ageless but how to live that way?

At Agape Church in Culver City, CA recently, I ran into an old friend now in his 70s, who lives free AND makes necessary adjustments. His life isn't on the layaway plan. He creates his current life based on his current realities. This fellow quit his job as a stockbroker at age 50. He divorced his wife of the time and reinvented. He now has a second home in Panama and a new wife. But what I've noticed over the 20 odd years I have known him is that he is always adjusting. He changes, but doesn't quit. A very athletic and fit man, he has done many extreme sports over the years (mostly free diving and ocean fishing), so I was shocked when he said he wouldn't be water skiing on a family trip to a lake. He said, 'I'll be watching this time due to my back prob-lems." He is modifying his behavior to deal with his new reality.

Accommodations because of physical changes are inevitable as we age. I denied pain in my back until there was no way and then quit running. The attitude of Mr. Panama is to stay connected and work around. Obsessing with aging is unproductive when it sucks out life and leaves you deflated. On the other hand, my soul wants to stay engaged. Aliveness wants out. I get it when making friends with younger people and doing new activities that require me to live in beginner mind.

After the concert at the Bowl, the crowd strolled out, singing the songs, and smiling like it was a new beginning. They had stepped out of age/class/race lines and roles and spent a few hours in the freedom of ageless, united, and positive spirits. Then they walked down the hill to their cars and buses and slipped back into the roles and personae of their daily lives. Separate souls but when the occasion comes together they are one or as Ziggy Marley sang, 'Love is my religion.' And I add, *ageless*.

Inner Journey:

☐ Think of a condition that you think limits your activities, your age, a physical or financial problem.

☐ Develop a work around. If you get stumped, then brainstorm with a friend.

Action Steps:

☐ On the street or at the market or at work, take the time to look at everyone that passes. What label to you immediately put on that person? Does it limit your experience or understanding of them?

Chapter 52
Is Your 'Spiritual, not Religious' Orthodox?

I don't believe in Beatles
I just believe in me
Yoko and me
And that's reality
—John Lennon, 1970

'You can't afford a negative thought.' 'All gossip is bad.' 'You can control conditions.' 'Prosperity is your divine right.' 'If you can dream it, you can achieve it.' Great slogans, motivational but beware, they may lead to magical thinking. These and many other nostrums have been sold to millions by spiritual teachers and self-help authors for over a century. One of the earliest of these platitudinous hucksters was James Allen's *As a Man Thinketh* (1902). During the Great Depression of the 1930s, desperate times attracted thousands to Napoleon Hill's *Think and Grow Rich*. In this tradition of positive thinking, in recent years *The Secret* Rhonda Byrne and *You Can Heal Your Life* by Louise Hay have been big hits.

Billions of dollars are made by promising that you can have anything you want. Adherents of these teachings are often refugees from religions that seemed stifling with dogmas such as good people get 'pie in the sky by and by' and bad people suffer weeping and wailing and gnashing of teeth down below. Some promoters of New Age culture also promise 'pie,' but this pie you can eat right here on earth, pretty seductive. But I prefer to live authentically right here and now, with all of its glory and the muck and the mire. Reality! What a concept.

In my case, I sampled the gifts of the New Age, but didn't buy it all. I had a pretty normal life. I pursued a professional career for almost thirty years, purchased my home with a mortgage, and paid for most everything in cash, pragmatic. Concurrently for thirty plus years, I walked the yellow brick road of the New Age. As a dedicated flower child of the Age of Aquarius, I found a spiritual home, positive lifestyle, and community. I lived in both worlds. You could say, I *rendered unto Caesar that which was of Caesar and that which was of god, spirit.*

How did I find this path? As a former Catholic and recovering Berkeley Marxist, my faith and hope was dim after college. The mid-70's was a time of cultural introspection and deflation in the aftermath of the Vietnam War. In a period of deep depression after a romantic break-up, I attended a transformational seminar, *est.* The rest is history, I joined the New Age with its amalgam of Eastern mysticism, pop psychology, and old fashioned American snake oil. A natural fit for someone coming out of the hippie/ radical movement of the sixties, it became my organizing principle: personal and spiritual growth. In this world I gained many deep friendships, personal insights, practical skills, and a lot of fun. But I saw the emperor wears no clothes.

New Age culture is largely based on ancient spiritual traditions that have proven the test of time. Sacred texts act as metaphorical teachings that are often applied to modern life. For some it is a half-way house between traditional religion and atheism. Definitely positive and helpful, but just as in traditional religion you'll find New Age **orthodox fundamentalism:** They often follow the latest fad, science and logic be damned, whether it be alkaline water or acai berry. Fads that cure everything that ails you. Evidence? Who needs science when you have anecdotal testimonial by a channeler or doctor of naturapathy?

Even Carl Jung, arguably the greatest psychiatrist of the 20th century, and on whose groundbreaking work many New Age theories are based, admitted that he was only modestly successful with clients two thirds of the time. He was not one to make grandiose and sweeping claims. Popular New Age author, Don Miguel Ruiz (*The Four Agreements* and other spiritual/self-help books) argues for careful analysis in his latest boo*k, The Fifth Agreement: Be Skeptical but Learn to Listen.*

The past few years have seen an explosion in popularity of these new/old ideas (*The Power of Now, Eat, Pray, Love*). Helpful and valuable, but like dessert, not sufficient for a healthy life. I am not saying that 'positive' thinking is bad or useless. Scientific studies indicate it is better to affirm, to expect the best, and to dream of a prosperous life (see Martin Seligman's *Authentic Happiness*). But even Seligman, the founder of positive psychology, has modified his views to include a range of attitudes, not just positive thinking. Literal New Agism may seduce the vulnerable into a fantasy world of goodness and light, where thinking, praying, and hoping is all it takes to get whatever you want.

I have known hundreds of 'seekers' in this counter-culture orthodoxy and most are sincerely seeking transformation, like me. 'If you can dream it, you can achieve it' asserts a popular nostrum. But those wise philosophers the Rolling Stones wrote back in

1969, 'You don't always get what you want, you get what you need.' Maturity has taught me to accept my life, and the conditions of it and at the same time work for inner and outer goals. And I know now that I won't get everything I want. That is how it works here on planet earth.

For a long time I had a smug self-righteousness, 'I am special because I am in this vanguard of 'consciousness.' Now, no longer an evangelist for the New Age, I am skeptical and curious, even of 'science.' As my close friend, the spoken word artist, Ravendove says, "Facts are changeable." I was a promulgator of these meatless notions, but now looking in the mirror with bare honesty and after too much denial, magical thinking, and disappointment, I see things differently—flabby thinking and platitudes be gone. I subject what I have gleaned from the New Age to the scrutiny of critical thinking. *Does it make sense? Is it effective? What is the evidence? What does my gut say?* Only then do I act and pay attention to my experience.

Sometimes the result look doesn't feel like heaven OR hell but in between, regardless, I practice *mindfulness*. Mostly, I remind myself **'keep your heart in the clouds and your feet on the ground.'**

Inner Journey:

☐ Where do you practice orthodoxy? Religion, politics, eating habits?

Action Steps:

☐ Spend a day mindful of your beliefs. Are you accepting advertising, heresay, or anecdotes as true without examination? Have a conversation of inquiry with a thoughtful friend.

Chapter 53
No More Questions or What Is Life?

*I love truth. I believe that man has need of it; but assuredly
he has still greater need of the illusions that encourage and
console...Rob him of his illusions and man would perish of
very weariness and despair.* —Anatole France

More powerful is he who has himself in his own power.
—Seneca

"How would you feel if at the end of your life you still had
questions?" Recently, a friend posed this hypothetical to me and
I shuddered. The quest to answer the riddle of life has been the
bane of my life, the big *WHY*? For decades I ardently pursued an
answer, as if life was a big game with a trophy at the end for
whoever toughs it out. Initially, like most spiritual seekers of my
generation, I turned to the East in my quest.

In July 1983 during a summer vacation, I went to Swami Muktananda's ashram in India. I had met him a couple years prior at
the famous big tent in Santa Monica. That evening I walked up to
the platform for a personal darshan (blessing), he mumbled
something in Hindi, then whacked me with a peacock feather, his
watery eyes drowning me in bliss. **I wanted whatever he had.**

Traveling around India severely tested my spirit and body, weakened from fighting dysentery for weeks, until like Alex in the seventies movie, *Clockwork Orange*, I stumbled into the Muktananda ashram at Ganeshpuri. The receptionist glared at me and said "Everyone does seva (service)."

Assigned to the kitchen cleaning the pots and pans, I pouted to myself—'I have two college degrees, I make good money on my job, and I'm too good for this.' Then one of the 'old timers,' a European man around 50, said, "Pots and pans is the seva of enlightenment." (*Yeh, right!*) The next morning I faced a stainless steel sink filled with pots and pans in a dark basement with only a sliver of light from a window. Remembering the purpose of my trip, I buckled down and grabbed the scrubber. By the end of that shift it hit me—*Everything was perfect just as it was*.

I got it, peace within was mine, and all I had to do was surrender my egoism and do what was in front of me. Unfortunately, my awakening was fleeting and I soon fell into my usual thoughts of judgment and separation. To this day, I still do not remember to stay present, I mostly live in the past, future, or distraction.

Recently my handyman (a country man from Trinidad), tossed me a zinger. In a rush to finish a remodeling project on my house, I spilled some paint. While methodically painting the wall he said, "Your impatience comes from not liking what you're doing and you want to get it over with and then make mistakes." How true! (pots in the ashram again) He continued, "Impatience becomes a habit, then nothing is good enough for your full attention and you're never satisfied." Bulls eye!

Many years ago in Thailand I encountered the happiest people in my many years of travel. Everyone I met from the taxi drivers to the shoe shiners to the prostitutes were smiling and laughing.

Thais are 90% Buddhist. In Buddhism, the basic teaching is *impermanence*, the cycle of life and death, endings and beginnings, everything evolving infinitely. Why is it so? Their answer? Because!

I finally ran out of questions and now believe answers are opinions anyway. So, what is left? Focus on the here and now and act—*live in the world*. Sometimes I lapse into futility, cynicism, and lethargy, but then I remember it's getting late—mature age adds urgency. At the same time, patience arises, *take it easy*. I've got nothing to prove and hold my goals and desires lightly. Once achieved a new one always appears to fuel action.

Each day my goal is to be present and aware and give thanks for things the way they are and keep 'why' to a minimum. Tomorrow is another day with mystery, challenge, and experience. I zigzag in the direction of my visions and goals, but whether I get there is not important. I put one step in front of the other and pay attention—no questions, just awareness and experience—Success!

Inner Journey:

☐ What is your concept of the meaning of life? Does it serve your happiness?

Action Steps:

☐ Practice mindfulness with some aversive task such as washing the dishes, doing your taxes, or whatever you actively don't like doing.

☐ Smile, play, & laugh for no reason for one day and then another day.

Everybody is a Star, No Matter Who You Are
—Sly & the Family Stone (Stone)

PART 10.
EXEMPLARS

Chapter 54
Ram Dass: His Message Is No Longer His Words

Everything has beauty, but not everyone sees it.
—Confucius

How far you go in life depends on your being tender with the young, compassionate with the aged, sympathetic with the striving, and tolerant of the weak and the strong, because someday in life you will have been all of these.
—George Washington Carver

A standing ovation by the audience of 150 in a yoga studio in Maui welcomed the noted spiritual seeker/teacher. His nickname was formerly Rent A Mouth, for his professional skill in story-telling. This night the stories were intact, but his speech was hampered. Due to stroke induced aphasia each word crossed over slowly from thought into speech. Although his concepts were lucid and clear, he labored articulating each word. A sentence unfolded ten times longer than normal speaking speed.

We heard tales of the old days at Harvard with his running bud of the time Tim Leary, and old chestnuts about Neem Karoli Baba, his guru. New tidbits about his long and very public life emerged from the winding road that is now his speech. He told his greatest hits, such as the time while tripping on LSD and he made a spectacle of himself in front of his parents shoveling snow in the middle of the night in the nude. Through it all, he weaved a cogent thread on spiritual liberation, through tales of his life over a twenty-five year period. After 45 minutes he had only gotten to 1970, and the moderator stepped in with a comment to the stone silent, but restless audience.

Carefully with much compassion and sensitivity, he suggested to the pin-drop silent room, "Noting that many of you are over forty-five or fifty, as I am, we are all going through a change in our physical bodies. We all have something doesn't work as it used to, be it sexuality, or a sore back or memory. We all share in the decline of the body, and our speaker highlights this aspect of life. Known for decades as a witty, insightful, engaging speaker, he now gives us a different gift."

There was some glancing about by members of the audience, a couple of persons got up and left, and the message of the day was emblazoned for me: *Compassion begins with the self.* Our generation's leading spiritual way-shower's latest message is not his anecdotes and accrued wisdom, it is in his example. He was on stage doing what he always did, entertaining and informing us, the first generation to seek spiritual enlightenment en masse. His ultimate teaching, and really what he always offered was his example of pushing to the next frontier. Whether it was with mind-expanding drugs or India with its yoga and meditation teachers, he was the avant-garde. That day from his tropical redoubt, he taught us about aging and death with his very public sharing of his challenges. Through it all he maintained his equanimity and humor, while revealing his ordinariness.

The natural order of life includes aging, with its inexorable physical decline. We have been a generation that made a cult of youth and our 'specialness.' Now no longer young, many want to hold onto youthfulness in spirit, appearance, and fitness. Let's try to stop time. Many years ago a hit record declared, 'all things must pass.' When I saw this icon with his very apparent aging, it awakened in me a strong sense of compassion, not for him, he is well in spirit. But for myself and my new back-ache, my new 24/7 glasses, and the older face in the mirror. Regard for the old teacher compelled me to pay attention to each carefully enunciated word and that effort forced mindfulness of the moment. The message was not the words or the space between the words but to my heart's deep desire for compassion for all beings, beginning with myself. Thank you Ram Dass, once again you have pointed the way.

Inner Journey:

☐ Remember and write about a time when you were impatient with someone with disabilities. How did you act?

☐ How do you feel when you are sick or unable to do normal tasks?

Action Steps:

☐ Find someone who is disabled or aged and provide a service they need.

☐ The next time your patience is tested in traffic, in a waiting room, or on a line: Be mindful.

Chapter 55
Art Kunkin: The Past Points to a Long Life

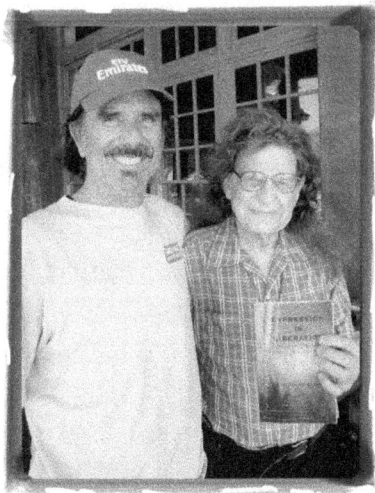

Be curious always. For knowledge will not acquire you. You must acquire it.   *—Sudie Back*

This, the aging process is worth celebrating. Chronological age marks how long you have lived but emotional age reflects what you have done with the time.
—Judith Sills

Returning to my favorite quick getaway recharge town in the Mojave Desert, Yucca Valley, I discovered a long-shuttered coffee lounge reopened. Minor structural and decor' changes have occurred but its' essential classic 40s architecture remains.

Pleasantly surprised after missing it for over a year, I bought my coffee and quiche and went outside to enjoy the warm desert air.

The day began with running into the annual Memorial Day parade on the main street, starring soldiers from the nearby 29 Palms Marine base. Slightly peeved at the delay, I did my ritual walk of the labyrinth at the *Joshua Tree Retreat Center*. After I saluted the seven directions at the medicine wheel, I drove to the intersection of 29 Palms Highway and Pioneertown Road. I intended to drive home the long way through Landers and eventually to *Deep Creek Hot Springs* for a long hike. But my tentative plan ran into a greater purpose.

Seeing a small man in his 80's in deep concentration on a book by L. Ron Hubbard, I shouted his name and introduced myself. For the next two hours we had a wide ranging, up to date conversation. This man is an iconic figure of the Sixties and legendary to my generation that came of age in Los Angeles then.

Art Kunkin published and edited one of the first and the most successful 'alternative' newspapers in the 60s and 70s, the *Los Angeles Free Press*. His influence as a promoter of the emerging hippie/radical culture can't be overstated. If you aspired to hipness at all (and what high school kid didn't) his rag was required reading. In it, I learned about the anti-war movement, protests in Berkeley, love-ins, *Hair* (the musical), concerts, and marijuana. I read poetry by Charles Bukowski, media criticism by Harlan Ellison, and excerpts from the *Pentagon Papers* by Daniel Ellsberg. In those pre-Internet days, access to current affairs was limited to the nine TV stations, the L.A. Times, and the throwaway papers. The excitement and tumult of the times was spread by newspapers such as the *Freep*, as it was affectionately known by its' fans. The *Free Press* announced the 'revolution.' By the late Sixties, its' weekly circulation reached over 100,000. The only other source of alternative information was Mort Sahl expounding radical views and interviews on local KHJ TV.

Craving more of this exciting and new culture, occasionally my buddies and I would make the 45 minute drive to Fairfax Ave in Hollywood and visit the Free Press bookstore. It stocked many hard to find items in 1967, candles, incense, radical books, black-light posters, beads, and bongs. When the crack in 1960's suburban-conformity widened and became an outright fissure in America, the *Free Press* and others like it were the harbingers of Dylan's *Times They Are a Changin.'* Too young to participate in the cultural and political tempests on the college campuses, we looked to Art Kunkin to keep us in the know.

Meeting this iconic and influential figure of the Sixties, reinforced my view that the mature stage of life offers the chance to renew and revive the spirit of our youth. The Sixties generation, had great hopes for real, significant change in our society. We know how that all turned out. My long ago optimism for social change got a boost talking with Kunkin. He is still in the vanguard. He spoke at length about his latest project, a technology for living up to 200 years of age. At 83, he is well versed on the latest advances in media and uses the Internet for disseminating his investigations of ancient alchemical teachings for life extension. The techniques can be read in detail on his website and in his weekly column. Not one to rest on his laurels, he is an exemplar of life-long growth, courage, and service.

As I left, Kunkin gave me with a useful tip: **meditate on the attributes of those that inspire you.** Art Kunkin influenced me from afar in my youth and now inspires me in person in my elder phase. He represents forward thinking that is not bound by age.

At 60, 70, 80 and more, life can be a journey of exploration, growth, and service. Looking at habits and comforts in my life and remembering the excitement of youth, my big take-away was *never stop learning and when you learn something, share it*. The second lesson of the day was to *trust my intuition* because it knows where I need to go. Although I missed my hike to Deep Creek Hot Springs, the synchronistic stop at the coffee lounge was as we used to say **right on time.**

Inner Journey:

☐ Recall one of the heroes of your youth. What appealed to you about them?

☐ How do those qualities resonate with you now?

Action Steps:

☐ Get a picture of that person and hang it on a wall or on the desk. Do some research and find out what they are up to now. Spend a week trying on those positive traits of your hero.

Chapter 56
Ravi Shankar's Magic Carpet of Passion and Youth

We work in the dark, we do what we can, we give what we have, our doubt is our passion, and passion is our task— the rest is the madness of art.

—Henry James

Most people are so busy knocking themselves out trying to do everything they think they should do, they never get around to do what they want to do.

—Kathleen Winsor

The familiar, high pitched voice welcomed the audience in his clipped Indian/English accent with self-effacing humility how we may not recognize him now with his long white beard. At 91, he is thin and walks with a cane and assistance, but once seated in the familiar cross-legged posture with his hands wrapped around the sitar, he exuded passion and energy with skill undiminished by time. Then weaving his spell with his sitar and the familiar sounding but unknown to this listener, ragas of India, the crowd instantly became still and silent.

A combination of concert, spiritual pilgrimage, and reunion of the tribe, the recital at Disney Hall in Los Angeles, seemed to be a miracle. Twice postponed, it stretched the mind that this unlikely avatar of our youth still played concerts. And play he did. He and his ensemble sat on carpets that we magically rode to a place that crossed the veil into the timeless, the eternal, and the unity of life. In the Sixties he opened a door to his world, and with the support of his since passed friend, George Harrison, helped a generation to discover world music. Never compromising in his fealty for authentic, classical Indian music, he enthralled us with his devotion and humor. On the *Concert for Bangladesh* album, the crowd applauds early on and he says "I hope you enjoy the concert as much as you did the tuning."

During this concert I kept having flashbacks to 1967 and his concert at the Hollywood Bowl that I attended as a teenager. At that concert, patchouli incense and cannabis sweetened the air and the transcendent mood. At the new Disney Hall in downtown L.A. (minus the fragrances and supported by an ensemble half his age), Raviji was just as vital and relevant as then.

Ravi has become more than a musician. His performance was more analogous to a saint or guru, but with no schtick (no hugs, no workshops, no obtuse philosophy), just his music. His depth of commitment to his art transcended the music. It exemplified the message of gurus, peace, harmony, and presence. He attracted an eclectic crowd with ample measures of old and young yogis in Indian prints, traditional dress suits and heels, and multi-generational Indian families dressed in saris and kurtas.

Ravi's music attracts individuals who step beyond the mainstream and into one of the rich tributaries of our global culture. Stronger than his music was Ravi's powerful passion. Undimmed by age and now seasoned by 75 years of performing, the music explored the etheric realms. His joy was infectious as he egged his musicians and the audience to new heights. He clearly lived to share his music and that passion taught much about a life well lived. His silent gift was his devotion to craft and art.

Seeing, hearing, and experiencing Ravi Shankar reminded me of sharing one's gift. It propels me now that I am in the last third of life, to uncover and then pursue it until it becomes a passion. A passion can become one's life purpose and as in the case of Raviji, his passion was a benediction for the world. Overtly, Shankar played music but the covert gift is the experience of harmony, self-expression, peace, and unity.

A career counselor, Richard Leider surveyed older adults to find out what makes them happy. He discovered that the prime factor is a sense of purpose and service in their lives. But many don't know how they can contribute. Uncovering and pursuing gifts and interests later in life can be our service and legacy. A talent not developed may deprive others of a rich legacy. But even more problematic, we maybe denying ourselves of the fulfillment that comes from living with passion at 91 or 81 or 61. I strive to drill down, discover, practice, and give away my gifts. Then like Ravi Shankar, perhaps I'll receive the boon of a life well-lived.

Inner Journey:

☐ Dive into your memory to recall a former passion that you gave up many years ago. Did you get bored of it or did you quit in frustration or some other reason?

Action Steps:

☐ If you were stumped on the above questions, try this for a few days: Before falling asleep, ask your unconscious to reveal a hidden passion.

☐ Do it, and give it a fair chance, no less than ten weeks of regular practice or experience.

Chapter 57
Casting a Wide Net Yields a Bountiful Life

*The key to immortality is first having a life worth
remembering.* —*Bruce Lee*

*Evolution and all hopes for a better world rest in the
fearlessness and open-hearted vision of people who
embrace life.* —*John Lennon*

None will improve your lot, if you yourself do not.
—*Bertolt Brecht*

The humming birds were buzzing around the bird feeder, while
she filled it with water and food. In a soft voice, she informed me
that they carried the spirits of her dead siblings and parents—
She was the only one still alive and they liked to visit. She is not
normally a superstitious type, but one day said "My mother used
to say to me hummingbirds were our dead relatives." Now, when
I sit in my backyard hot tub and the hummingbirds fly around
and I think of departed family, usually Uncle Toot.

Committed to a full life, this older lady defines involvement and
creative expression. Her typical day is, check the stock market, go
to water color painting or exercise class, garden in her yard, play
bridge in the evening, and then 'stream' a movie. Keeping this
schedule day in, day out would be daunting for someone half her
age. But she doesn't stop, and barely takes time for the occasional

nap. "Why would I stop? If I did, I may as well die," she says.

One day I asked her about the meaning of life. She responded, "Look around. What do you see?—Plants, animals, nature. That is what it is about." No concepts, no theories of the hereafter, and no god, just the simple expression of life with all of its abundance. In her garden, last year's roses and tomatoes are long gone. Like her career in public education, that was then and she moved on. 'Let the dead bury the dead.'

Born and raised in a small New England town, this skinny, big brown eyed, dark-haired daughter of Italian immigrants had an overarching dream—live life in all its fullness. Never one for sitting still, as a small child she would follow her older brothers where ever they went—wanting to explore the world. That inclination stayed with her in moving to California with her Navy officer, later civil engineer husband, living in Europe for a couple years in the Sixties, traveling to foreign lands nearly every summer vacation, and even more often in 'retirement.

At 62 she retired from a career in teaching elementary school, but not from life. Immediately she began taking art classes ranging from abstract painting to sculpture to watercolors. Befuddling her instructors with her wild creativity, she would turn a simple ceramic pot into phantasmagoria of shapes out of the *Lord of the Rings*. Once a skill is learned, she moves on to a new one. It didn't matter if she was 65 or 75 or even 85. Learning and exploring is the gold of life for her. She transformed herself just as she did the back yard of her house from basic grass and concrete into a verdant collection of colorful native and drought tolerant plants.

Not confined to travel, gardening, and art, her smorgasbord of interests includes mental stimulation as well. About a year ago, she began to learn chess along with her other recent interests in *Sudoku* and *RummyKube*. I don't know what happened to chess, but I suspect it got lost in her re-surging popularity as a contract bridge player. That takes about three to four days per week. There is only so much time.

She also found an outlet for her teaching skills by volunteering at the local library. Once per week she assists adults improve their reading and writing skills. In that role she often becomes a surrogate mother, offering gentle counsel along with correcting grammar.

When I look at this woman in her mid eighties, I see the young girl who wanted to experience the world and life. Not limited by her ethnicity, small town upbringing, poverty, or discrimination, she has seized opportunities. Always busy, she took college classes at night while raising three children. But it is in her 'retirement' years that she has really shined.

Never one for fancy things: for her life is for living, not possessions. Recently, she found some old family photos in a back closet. They had been sent to her when her last brother died and she hadn't looked at them. We leafed through the mixed collection of wedding, army, and school photos and she named relatives captured in moments forty, sixty, one hundred years ago. A mystery was solved for me. I got a clue to what fuels her relentless zeal for living. It is an unbreakable family bond: A rock solid foundation that remains and sustains her through all of the travels, classes, friends, and hobbies.

Although she left her hometown to live her life 3,000 miles distant, she never left her family *and* she was not limited by her family. Their love and support seems to have inspired her wide ranging interests and creative expressions. Her guiding principles are not planned, not studied, not counseled but they are authentic, **be curious, learn new skills, give back to society, be close to nature, and remember the past but live in the present.**

She is not without struggles or faults, but she is real. My mother is my greatest teacher about this stage of my life. Finding satisfaction and fulfillment in older age is often difficult and I believe calls for freedom, courage, and curiosity. It is not easy or automatic. But I know at least one success story— Belinda Zompa Klarin, an exemplar of forging organic, maximum living after 'retirement.' More than reinventing, she casts a wide net on the sea of life and makes the most of whatever she catches.

Inner Journey:

☐ Take time to reflect on the lifestyles of elderly persons you have known personally. What did they do and think? Were they content and fulfilled?

Action Steps:

☐ Find an elderly (over 80) person who seems content and fulfilled, and interview them.

☐ Do something new that expands your current lifestyle.

Chapter 58
Bob Marley's Quest for Universal Redemption

One day the years of struggle will strike as the most beautiful. —*Sigmund Freud*

You are not here to merely make a living. You are here in order to enable the world to live more amply, with greater vision, with a finer spirit of hope and achievement. You are here to enrich the world . . . —*Woodrow Wilson*

At an outside table, in the bright sunlight, in front of the coffee house my close friend and occasional writing partner, Ravendove, popped a big question. "Did you see it? He was on a mission." He couldn't wait to discuss a new film. I responded, "Yes, I had a few friends over and we all celebrated the man and his music. He was this era's prophet." We were referring to the documentary on Bob Marley's life, *Marley*. As a lifelong fan and student of Marley, I highly recommend the film for both the uninitiated and veteran Marleyites. His epic story is well told and includes new info and never before filmed associates and lovers. Marley was a man on a mission of redemption for mankind: *One love, one heart, one destiny.*

Are you on a mission or quest? Life as a quest is not for everyone, but for those who feel the call it there is no option. Questers are history's game changers, the people who have impacted us all. Reflecting on the direction of my life in retirement, I've had moments of wondering if I need to take on a big purpose. Doubt surfaced and the thoughts arose, 'Maybe there is an easier way?' 'Perhaps I can develop a lifestyle that fulfills and is easy and just fun.' 'Do I really need a quest?' Then the famous Howard Thurman quote came to mind, "Stand before me in my moments of weakness my high resolve." The path of courage and purpose knows no other way.

Ravendove continued, "After seeing it my wife said she finally got me. She knows what moves me now. He was driven, he had no choice. It wasn't a matter of morality or emotions. He had to live that way. And Rita Marley, Bob's wife, supported him in the mission."

I agreed and replied, "The mission was more important than maintaining a conventional home life." Consider Bill and Hillary Clinton, Hillary supported Bill, not in a blind 'stand by your man' way, but because of the work. 20th Century examples abound where a charismatic leader's mission overrode personal morality. Towering figures of the twentieth century come to mind from Thomas Edison to FDR to Gandhi to Martin Luther King, Jr. In that vein, Howard Thurman said that a person's mission is of primary importance and then comes his mate.

Biographies of iconic leaders reveal the power of living a big question. How can I serve? For true leaders, service inevitably calls them to a mission. The mission flows through their 'god given talent.' *Marley*, clearly showed how he was driven to serve by sharing his musical gifts. Not philosophy from a book or heard at a seminar, Marley shared his life's struggles and joys in his songs. His early life of poverty, of being half-caste, and father abandonment fueled his talent. He pursued his need for acceptance by digging for a deeper truth—universal brotherhood. Nothing could stop him. He worked for it tirelessly for several years even while the cancer that killed him spread through his body. He left this life with the question still on his lips: How can I bring people together?

Joseph Campbell, renowned mythologist, said we all have a quest inside of us. But most are unconscious of that mission, and stay satisfied with low level goals like making more money, having more pleasure, or just comfort seeking. Uncovering a bigger question and consciously living that way may be the ultimate liberation for the Boomer in retirement. Now, no longer dependent on external demands such as raising a family and a career, the quest can truly begin in earnest. What excites? What fulfills? What stretches? What brings peace of mind? Ultimately, how can I contribute and grow?

A personal quest never ends and constantly morphs. Each step leads to the answer, but also the next question. Discovering one's purpose takes more than study. The hero's journey is offered to all, but not all heed the call, according to Campbell in his seminal book *The Hero with a Thousand Faces (1949)*.

But the questions don't stop and nor should they. Every answer or achievement is provisional because it leads to another question. To expect to reach the end of life without questions is hubris. When we get to an end something new immediately arises. Knowing that basic truth and accepting it may open the door to peace of mind.

For me, the quest goes on. When I am at that last rest stop, I hope to look back and see that I have responded to my inner questions and accepted the missions that led to new questions. Then a new and bigger question can arise, 'What is next?'

Inner Journey:

☐ Did you ever have a great vision of helping the world? Have you done so?

☐ Please list any regrets about how the world has changed in your adult lifetime.

Action Steps:

☐ Scan your immediate world for things that need to be changed, then make a plan to help.

☐ Be the change by volunteering time, donating money, or publicizing the issue.

EPILOGUE

Sitting in a sunlight sidewalk café, in a newly gentrified section of Los Angeles, I am living my dream. Not the dream I expected, but the one that evolved. I am busy putting the finishing touches on this book, planning an adventure trip, and signing up for classes in tango. I got up this morning on my own schedule, and took plenty of time to ease into the day. Without the consuming career, my dreamscape has expanded to include virtually any place in the world and doing almost anything. I have reinvented and expanded into a world view that feels unlimited.

What's next? Like an exciting journey, I've changed a lot since the beginning of these essays. In this book, you've had a opportunity to peek into my inner and outer world as I grappled with life-defining questions. I hope that some of it resonates with you personally. And I am sure other parts, not so much.

Seven years have now passed since my graduation from the Monday through Friday job/career, ups and downs, expansion and contraction, creativity and depression, all traveled with me on this journey of exploration. Curiosity led me to inner and outer places of unexpected wonder and terror. In the process,

I gave up outdated fantasies about retirement. Now each day is an adventure of the soul and the body.

After five or six decades of living, most Boomers have probably seen that when one goal is achieved or a certain issue handled, another one appears. The cliché holds: *Life is not a destination but a journey*. There is no final, ultimate success—there is always another mountain to climb. Our goals motivate us, but life consists of beginnings and endings. Diving into the mystery of life again and again takes courage, but I can think of nothing more important or satisfying.

Each of us has a hero within. When resuscitated, the hero faces obstacles inside and out that we want to take on. The challenge is to face one's unique growing edge that calls out for recognition, growth, and expression, which may have been avoided for many years, but is simply dormant. But following that call yields its own reward of inner peace, self-acceptance, and contentment. LIVING the dream.

On my hero's journey, demons and angels both appeared. Early on, I looked long and deep my personality, my lifestyle, and my community. Many questions arose again and again: Who am I? What is it all about? How do I find satisfaction in this moment? Who are my friends and fellow-travelers? Where am I going? And the big one, 'What is this thing called life?' These and countless other questions emerged, after I had exchanged suit and ties and haircuts for jeans, t-shirts, and a ponytail.

I turned in my school keys and completed my exit paperwork and expected a dreamland without bells. Little did I know I had leapt into an unknown river without a paddle and landed in spinning eddies of the 'real' world. The world's message to me was, 'you've got a pension and the rest will take care of itself.'

As if retirement is like sex—it just comes naturally, so don't worry about it. But like sex for most of us, there is a lot more to it than jumping into bed. It was much tougher transition than I thought.

Similar to graduating from college, retiring was a new beginning filled with similar angst and questions—'What do I want to do?,' 'Where do I want to live?,' 'Who do I want to be with?' One author calls it, "adding life after subtracting work." Gratefully, the new college graduate's concern for an income was absent for me. It forced me to become more intrinsically motivated.

Sometime between my Death Valley wilderness vision quest, and the second two week trip to Maui, that new issues arose with aging. I didn't just bliss-out floating downstream. I had to get in the boat and grab the paddle and figure out how to negotiate the whitewater rapids and whirlpools, while avoiding the hidden rocks in the river. As the ancient oracle, the *I Ching*, says, 'Water can't be stopped, but it can be guided.'

Confused about my purpose and direction, one day I stopped by my old elementary school and something burst. I got it. Tears of relief and joy flowed freely. I said to my girlfriend, "I don't know where this is coming from but it is real." Then it hit me. In sixth grade, I had won the school-wide essay contest, which resulted in a story in the local paper. At that point, I realized I needed to write. I started a blog, *SM Babylon*, where I ranted about political goings on in my town and published some poetry. Creative expression became my liberation. Partly, for my own clarity and healing, I blogged *Living the Dream Deferred.*

Within each of us is a creative spark that wants expression regardless of whether we are naturally talented or not. By expressing my inner feelings, thoughts, and desires, I discovered a reality that eventually and continually births a new experience of life. Pursuing reinvention requires courage, the heart to keep "keeping on" in this strange, different phase of life. But the Creative rewards its suitor with full-on living.

No longer *living the dream deferred,* I've crossed the great water to a new land and a new me. No longer fitting into a suit too small, my daily life emerges organically from the core. There are still hills and valleys, but now I embrace it all. I found no dreamland over the rainbow, but I gained acceptance and satisfaction in life right now.

May be you'll take that first step in discovering and living your dreams, and perhaps that on that last breath you can say with me: **My dreams are no longer deferred. I have done what I came here for... I have taken my journey of adventure, expression, and discovery... I am well pleased ... I am satisfied ... What a wild, wacky, and wonderful trip it's been.**

APPENDIX:

The 5 As: *A technology to support living your dream*

If you have gotten this far, perhaps my meandering reports from the frontline of **Boomer** reinvention have touched something in you. That something may be called the creative spirit, god, higher power, or a myriad of other labels—which are not the thing itself. Your interiority is not my interiority, but they may have elements in common. And in that commonality, my personal strategy may be useful in your journey to *living **your** dream deferred.*

From the beginning my intention was to provide a helpful tool for others in similar circumstances: retirement from a structured career and desiring a free and expressive life. As noted in the epilogue, my beliefs changed over the course of writing these essays and I no longer believe that success of any type can be scripted. Purveyors of self-help techniques that promulgate easy, guaranteed solutions are the modern snake oil salesmen. Take my word for it, I've done most of them.

In many of the essays, I cited psychological theories that I have become familiar with, ranging from Jung's synchronicity and *Red Book*, to Deci and Ryan's *Self Determination Theory,* to Sufi's zikr, to David Allen's productivity principles, to Ernie Zelinski's 'Happy, Wild, & Free,' to Werner Erhard's *Landmark Forum*, to Ernest Holmes' *Science of Mind* to Adwin Brown's *Flownation*. Each offers useful tools for creatively reinventing one's life. They complemented my 25 year practice of vipassana meditation, which in true 21st century 'spiritual (not religious) fashion, provides the ground from which my other practices spring.

In the material below, which I call the *5As*, I offer an outline to guide your exploration into your authentic, creative, free self—the self that flourishes in all dimensions of life.

Before I describe my *5As*, a slight side trip is needed. The founder of positive psychology, Martin Seligman, defines a successful or flourishing life as one that is satisfying in five dimensions which he refers to as **PERMA—Pleasurable** emotions, **Engagement** or passion, positive **Relations**, **Meaning** or purpose, and **Achievement** or growth. At times many people feel a vague unease without being able to pinpoint something wrong. He suggests that when this happens, it means that one or more of these domains needs some development. This is where my *5As* come in.

The *5As* are **Awareness, Acceptance, Action, Appreciation, and Assessment**. These terms grew out of my analysis and implementation of projects that came to a successful conclusion. Like Seligman, I noticed that when something in me was stuck, spinning around, or confused, one of the *5As* needed attending. It became a loose framework for me to keep track of my visions and goals.

Awareness: Awareness is another way of saying be present to what is, either in the moment, in past experience, or future vision. Much of our emotional life is cluttered with regrets about the past or anxiety of the future. Those times don't exist. The only time is now. But that doesn't mean the past or future is irrelevant. In fact awareness of how past experiences contributed to this moment and clarity of intent for the future enhances skillfulness now. Taking time to see what was, is, and what may be provides valuable data on which to make discerning decisions. Sometimes the vision is too occluded, and then an expert (friend, therapist, or coach) may helpful.

Acceptance: Sometimes when we become aware of something, denial sets in—'that can't be,' 'no way' and so on. At these times, look at the big picture. You've had other trials and tribulations and yet have survived or prospered. When we don't accept what is going on within and without, we miss the data that help us make course adjustments. Aircraft and spaceships must constantly make micro adjustments, and the same goes for the frustrations, insecurities, and mistakes that occur when we choose to live proactively.

Action: Too often we procrastinate around goals. Taking action is aversive for some reason: difficult, tedious, or painful, but not acting allows the universe to determine your fate. This is not to say we have control over everything that occurs to us, but we can influence and make our best effort in the direction or trajectory of our goals. Study, meditation, reflection are all valuable tools but they rarely substitute for conscious, focused activity for getting results.

Appreciation: On a purely karmic level, appreciation is important. Positive things tend to get set in motion when gratitude is in the space. For the individual, good feelings accrue within, when we give thanks. Serotonin excretes in the brain and happiness increases. Studies have shown that the happiest people are the most grateful.

Assessment: *Related to but not the same as awareness, assessment is a careful examination of the results of one's actions. A kind of non-judgmental 'how did I do?' or 'what specifically happened' it provides information necessary to learn from the experience and make good decisions on how to proceed.*

The **5As** are not a belief system or philosophy; they simply offer you an outline to keep on track in this highly distracting and cacophonous world today. Specific tools to assist the application of the **5As** are offered in my workshops and personal coaching. Above all, remember that this world is a laboratory and we're all experimenting.

May you keep flowing!

BIBLIOGRAPHY

Aging/Reinvention

Bolles, Richard & Nelson, John, *What Color is Your Parachute—for Retirement: Planning Now for the Life You Want.* Ten Speed Press, 2007

Bridges, William, *The Way of Transitions: Embracing Life's Most Difficult Moments.* Perseus Publishing, 2001

Dass, Ram, *Still Here Now: Embracing Aging, Changing, and Dying*. Riverhead Books, 2000

Frankl, Viktor, *Man's Search for Meaning: An Introduction to Logotherapy.* Beacon Press, 1959

Hillman, James, *The Force of Character: And the Lasting Life*. Random House, 1999

Jarow, *The Ultimate Anti-Career Guide: The Inner Path to Finding Your Work in the World* (audiobook). Sounds True, 2004

Lawrence-Lightfoot, Sara, *The Third Chapter: Passion, Risk, and Adventure in the 25 Years After 50*. Sarah Crichton Books, 2009

Richmond, Lewis, *Aging as a Spiritual Practice: A Contemplative Guide to Growing Older and Wiser.* Gotham Books, 2012

Williamson, Marianne, *The Age of Miracles: Embracing the New Midlife.* Hay House, 2008

Zelinski, Ernie, *How to Retire Happy, Wild, and Free: Retirement Advice You Won't Get from Your Financial Advisor.* Visions International Publishing, 2011

Creativity

Booth, Eric, *The Everyday Work of Art: Awakening the Extraordinary in Your Daily Life.* iUniverse.com, 2001

Martinez, Ruben, *Desert America: Boom and Bust in the New Old West.* Henry Holt and Co., 2012

May, Rollo, *The Courage to Create.* Norton, 1975.

Pressfield, Steven, *The War of Art: Break Through the Blocks and Win Your Creative Battles,* Black Irish Entertainment, 2002

Osho, *Creativity: Unleashing the Forces Within.* St Martin's Press, 1999

Tharp, Twlya, *The Creative Habit: Learn It and Use It for Life.* Simon & Schuster, 2003

Writing

Cameron, Julia, *The Right to Write: An Invitation and an Initiation into the Writing Life.* Jeremy Tarcher/Putnam, 1998

Hemley, Robin, *A Field Guide for Immersion Writing: Memoir, Journalism, and Travel.* University of Georgia Press, 2012

Keyes, Ralph, *The Courage to Write: How Writers Transcend Fear.* Henry Holt & Co, 1995

Lopate, Phillip, *To Show and To Tell: The Craft of Literary Nonfiction.* Free Press, 2013

Mailer, Norman, *The Spooky Art: Thoughts on Writing.* Random House, 2003

Schneider, Pat, *Writing Alone and with Others.* Oxford University Press, 2003

Shapiro, Michael ed., *A Sense of Place: Great Travel Writers Talk about Their Craft, Lives, and Inspiration.* Traveler's Tales, 2004

Sher, Gail, *One Continuous Mistake: Four Noble Truths for Writers.* Penguin, 1999

Theroux, Paul, *The Tao of Travel: Enlightenments from Lives on the Road.* Mariner Books, 2012

Self Management/Development

Allen, David, *Ready for Anything: 52 Productivity Principles for Getting Things Done.* Penguin, 1999.

—— *Getting Things Done: The Art of Stress-free Productivity.* Penguin, 2001

Covey, Stephen R., *7 Habits of Highly Effective People: Restoring the Character Ethic.* Fireside Books, 1990

Deci, Edward & Ryan, Richard, *Self-Determination Theory and the Facilitation of Intrinsic Motivation, Social Development, and Well-being,* American Psychologist, V.55

Polard, Andrea, *A Unified Theory of Happiness: An East Meets West Approach to Fully Loving Your Life.* Sounds True, 2012

Osho, *Intuition: Knowing Beyond Logic.* St Martin's Press, 2001

Schwartz, Barry, *The Paradox of Choice: Why More Is Less.* Harper-Collins, 2004

Ruiz, Don Miguel, *The Four Agreements: A Practical Guide to Personal Freedom.* Amber-Allen Publishing, 1997

—— *The Fifth Agreement: A Practical Guide to Self-Mastery.* Amber-Allen Publishing, 2011.

Seligman, Martin, *Flourish: A Visionary New Understanding of Happiness and Well Being & Authentic Happiness.* Free Press, 2011

—— *Authentic Happiness: Using the New Positive Psychology to Realize Your Potential for Lasting Fulfillment.* Free Press, 2002

Inspiration

Cole-Whitaker, Terry, *What You Think of Me Is None of My Business,* Oak Tree Publications, 1979

Coelho, Paulo, *The Alchemist: A Fable About Following Your Dream.* HarperCollins, 1988

Hafez trans. by Daniel Ladinsky, *The Gift.* Penguin, 1999

Hillman, James, *The Soul's Code: In Search of Character and Calling.* Random House, 1996

Jung, CG, *The Red Book—Liber Novus,* W.W. Norton & Co., 2009

—— *Memories, Dreams, Reflections.* Random House, 1961

—— *Synchronicity: An Acausal Connecting Principle.* Bollingen Foundation, 1952

More, Thomas, *Dark Night of the Soul: A Guide to Finding Your Way through Life's Ordeals.* Penquin, 2004

Osho, *Courage: The Joy of Living Dangerously.* St Martin's Press, 1999

Osho, *Osho Zen Tarot.* St Martin's Press, 1994

Robinson, Joe, *Don't Miss Your Life: Find More Joy and Fulfillment Now.* Jon Wiley & Sons Inc., 2011

Rumi, Jelaludin trans. by Coleman Barks, *The Essential Rumi.* HarperCollins, 1995

Wilhem, Richard trans. Baynes, Cary, *The I Ching or Book of Changes.* Princeton Univ. Press, 1950

Miscellaneous Citations

Coppola, Francis Ford (director), *Apocalypse Now* (movie). 1979

Estevez, Emilio (director), *The Way* (movie). 2011

Gersh-Young, Marjorie, *Hot Springs and Hot Pools of the South-west.* Aqua Thermal Access, 2011

Holmes, Ernest, *The Science of Mind.* Dodd, Meade, & Co., 1938

Kazantsakis, Nikos, *Zorba the Greek.* Simon & Schuster, 1952

Klages, Ellen, *Harbin Hot Springs: Healing Waters, Sacred Land.* Harbin Springs Publishing, 1993

Kunkin, Art, *The Los Angeles Free Press.* 1964-1978

McDonald, Kevin (director), *Marley* (movie). 2012

Marley, Bob, *Exodus (music album).* Tuff Gong/Island, 1977.

Pink Floyd, *Atom Heart Mother (music album).* Capitol Records, 1970

Porter, Donald & Taxson, Diane, *The est Experience.* Award Books, 1976

Shankar, Ravi, *Concert for Bangladesh (music album).* Apple Records, 1971

Wehrheim, John, *Taylor Camp.* Serendia Contemporary, 2009

Stone, Robert (director), *Taylor Camp: 1969-1977 They created order without rules . . . a clothing-optional, grow your own tree house village at the end of Kauai (movie).* 2010

White, John Wythe, *High and Beautiful Wave: It Was a Great Ride while It Lasted.* Mutual Publishing, 2008

Works by friends who have Reinvented:

Basson, Gert, (financier/business development), *The Fourth Reich (movie),* 1990.

Brooks, Herman (medical doctor), *Unity Posse (music album).* Raj-jahz Productions, 2012

Brown, Adwin David (poet), *Angel City Blues: (multi-media experience)* 2014

Buchanan, Denise (landscape architect), *The Sins of the Fathers: A True Story of Rape and Deception in the Catholic Church and . . . Spiritual Renewal.* Lulu Press, 2012

Chandonnet, Jon (software engineer), *Shadow Summit: One Man, His Diagnosis, and the Road to a Vibrant Life.* Vibrant Living Press, 2013

Cheng, Fu-Ding (architect/graphic design), *Map of Desire,* Liquid Light Productions, 2014

Dowell, Ron (accountant/L.A. County) *Compton 4 Cops: Community-Based Crime Fighting in Disadvantaged Racially and Ethnically Diverse Urban Communities.* Outskirts Press, 2011

Finch, Anthony (gadfly), *A Road High and Low.* Xlibris, 2000

Pogue, Leslie (administrative assistant) *28 Days to Happy.* Create Space, 2011 and *Positive Side of Bad Stuff.* Create Space, 2013

Pray, William F (teacher), *What Can I Do? Ethics and the Situation.* Rhino Publications, 2011

BIOGRAPHY

R.W. Klarin worked as teacher, dean of discipline, assistant principal, principal, and headquarters administrator in a nearly thirty year career in education. Concurrent with his career with the Los Angeles Unified School District, he pursued myriad spiritual/ personal growth paths from Advaita to Zen for almost 33 years.

Born in Los Angeles and raised in the San Fernando Valley, he has been a resident of the Ocean Park district of Santa Monica since 1974. Even though he advocates life and creative expression as the greatest teachers, he has acquired two graduate degrees and a BA with a total of 10 years of seat time in higher education (UC Berkeley, Cal State Northridge, National University, LMU, and Southwestern Law School). Klarin has travelled to over 50 countries and visited over 100 hot springs, exhibited a solo art show, published a book of poetry and a book of essays, and dabbled in numerous creative happenings/ events.

Current projects include columns, books, videos, and coaching on courage, hot springs, and reinvention. He may be reached at rwklarin@yahoo.com or www.livingthedreamdeferred. com or www.rwklarin.com.

www.ingramcontent.com/pod-product-compliance
Lightning Source LLC
Chambersburg PA
CBHW020923090426
42736CB00010B/1014